Acclaim for **Jacqueline Wale**

THE FEAR

MW00696222

"Jacqueline Wales gets right down to the heart of our fears—that we're getting older, that we're "on the other side of the hill," that perhaps we blew it and we'll never have a chance to get it right this lifetime—and uses a magician's touch to turn such thoughts around. THE FEARLESS FACTOR shows us a blazing light at the end of all those worries. I found myself nurtured by every chapter I read, and it made me happy to think of how many women Jacqueline is helping, and will help in the days to come. It's a really good read."—**Marianne Williamson, author of** *The Age of Miracles and The Gift of Change*

"Often people let fear hold them back from intelligent choices, but it doesn't have to be that way. In Jacqueline Wales' new book, The Fearless Factor, she says being fearless is about the choices and decisions we make in life and her compelling life story will inspire you to move past the ghosts of the past and venture into an entirely new world where you will never allow yourself to be victimized again by fear! I highly recommend this book."—**Lee Milteer, author of** *Success Is An Inside Job—Spiritual Power Tools*

"Jacqueline Wales has offered an outstanding resource to not only identify and define your fears, but offers solid solutions for eliminating them as an obstacle in your path to greatness."—**Carla Harris, author of** *Expect to Win*

"Fear is our essential lack of belief in our ability to handle whatever comes our way. Full of wonderful anecdotes and heart-felt stories, Jacqueline Wales beautifully illustrates how to start managing your fears so you can live your life the way you want it to be."— **Susan Jeffers, Ph.D., author of** *Feel the Fear and Do It Anyway®* **and** *Life is Huge!*

"Mention the word fear and some people head for the hills. In this intriguing book, author Jacqueline Wales introduces a new, refreshingly healthy approach that shows how to put fear to work FOR us rather than AGAINST us. In tough economic times, we all need to know how to fast-forward through fear instead of becoming frozen by fear. This book shows how anyone can do that. Read it and reap."—**Sam Horn, author of** *POP!, Tongue Fu!* **and** *What's Holding You Back?*

"If you want to step fearlessly into a bold new world of your doing, then get this book! It will take you step by step and catapult you toward success."
—**Stephanie Frank, author of** *The Accidental Millionaire*

"This book is a 'must read' for every woman who wants to be all that she can be. NOW! Don't' wait! Read this book NOW!"—**Margot Anand, author of** *The Art of EveryDay Ecstasy*

"If you are looking to thrive beyond "the jungle" of your life, then read what Jacqueline Wales has to offer in her wonderful new book. It will lead you on the path towards your own transformation."—**Al Secunda, author of** *The 15-Second Principle*

"They say a teacher or a book will appear when the student is ready, The Fearless Factor is that book. Jacqueline's journey is inspiring. Her passion to share and teach her fearless message, powerful and direct."—**Mary Ann Halpin, Photographer for Fearless Women: Midlife Portraits**

"In the Fearless Factor, Jacqueline's honesty, compassion and wisdom shine through and it is clearer than ever that we have a choice every day to make a life of love or to live a life of fear."—**Annie Teich, The Teich Group**

We all have a jungle inside our head that we must travel through to discover the essence of who we are, and in this personal and powerful book, Jacqueline Wales illustrates how we can all create the life we want if we are willing to step beyond the limitations of our fears, doubts and anxieties."—**Bonnie St John, author of *Live Your Joy*, Amputee, Olympic ski medalist, and inspirational speaker.**

We spend our lives searching for answers, yet frequently don't ask the right questions in order to find them. The Fearless Factor asks lots of questions, and the answers may well surprise you. Read this book when you are serious about moving beyond the fears that stop you from living your best life now."—**Andrea Nierenberg, author of *Million Dollar Networking: The Sure Way to Find, Grow and Keep Your Business***

"In this book for the times, Jacqueline Wales has clearly defined what we can do to go beyond the fear, doubts and anxieties that stop us from living our best life. She illustrates beautifully the power of choice made by women who meet the challenge and embrace being fearless."—**Loral Langemeier-Bestselling author of *The Millionaire Maker* 3-book series and CEO of Live Out Loud**

"Is your fear creating excess "baggage" that holds you back? Jacqueline Wales will take you on a journey to discover how courageous you can truly be as you move past the fears, doubts and anxieties, and truly embrace the essence of YOU."—**Casey Wohl, author of *The Girls Getaway Guide* series**

"Jacqueline Wales says fear is a normal part of our existence, but the challenge is in recognizing that it is a powerful motivating force as well. Through the stories and questions asked in this book, you will find the motivation to overcome your own fears. This is a must-read for anyone who has ever wanted to live a more fulfilled life."—**Linda Seger, author of *Spiritual Steps on the Way to Success***

"We all face fears, it's part of being human and our evolution of personal growth. HOW we choose to FACE those fears makes the difference. In The Fearless Factor, Jacqueline Wales shows us handle to handle our fears, self-doubts and anxieties, to minimize reactions with new survival skills that maximize our confidence. Both the format and the content of this book is easy to read and nurturing to your soul."—**Sheryl Roush, Author of *Heart of a Woman*, and inspirational speaker**

THE FEARLESS FACTOR

OVERCOME THE FEARS, DOUBTS, AND ANXIETIES THAT STOP YOU FROM BEING YOUR BEST SELF NOW

Jacqueline Wales

May,

You Are Fearless!

With love
Jacqueline

The Fearless Factor

Published by Turning Point Press
8 E.127th Street
New York, NY 10035

The Fearless Factor is a trademark of Jacqueline Wales

ISBN: 0979859816
EAN-13: 9780979859816

Books may be ordered at www.TheFearlessFactor.com

Layout by ABCwriters.com

Printed in the United States of America

To my family who taught me all I needed to know about becoming FEARLESS. Without you on the journey, I would have been lost.

Notes

Table Of Contents

Part 1
Enter the Jungle

CHAPTER 4

CHAPTER 5

Part 2
Choose the Right Path

CHAPTER 6

Chapter 7

Chapter 8

Chapter 9

Chapter 10

Part 3
Arrive at the Clearing

Chapter 15

Part 4
Master the Jungle

Chapter 16

Chapter 17

Chapter 18

ACKNOWLEDGEMENTS

W e are never alone on these journeys through the jungle of life, and have many teachers along the way. I have been blessed for many years with wise and profound women to guide me on my path. There are many people who have assisted and supported me in achieving my vision towards creating this book. I especially want to thank Lauren Powers, who helped me understand I had a much bigger game to play than the one I had originally intended and brought me into the world of coaching. Stephanie Frank for being a wise counselor in business and in life, who encouraged me to realize my vision of creating a foundation for success that would help inspire women all over the world to seek their own dreams and live them. Thanks also to Amy Collins for her love, her support and heart, Bethany Brown, who believed in my message and made me look good on paper and Frank Rivera for being a truly great book designer. Their help has been invaluable in bringing you this book you have in your hand.

To the many women who have entered my life over the years, you are my true inspiration. You have brought me your wisdom and your love, and I have learned to write my truth and express it with your stories. To the Fearless women who contributed essays to the book, I thank you all for being true examples of women with the courage to change. To all of you, your strength has become my strength, and together we grow into beautiful examples of women who live their own lives. We are indeed sisters on the same road.

I want to thank the experts I have learned from over the years. Their analysis of fear, and the various techniques you can use to move yourself out of fear and into fearless have been invaluable. I have been lucky to study master teachers who brought their gift to the world and helped make it mine. I take full responsibility for my interpretation of your work.

We live our life in relationship to others, and I've been blessed with a partner who has challenged me and loved me more than anyone else on this planet. My husband Martin, has been with me through the many ups and downs of my life for over twenty-nine years. His support has encouraged me to keep the faith and believe I could do anything I wanted...and I have. And my children—who are no longer children but four young adults—are as much a blessing as anyone could hope to have. They are fine examples of people living their own fearless lives. Robert in England, Virginia in Thailand, Serena in Boston, and Samara in New York, you are the light of my existence. Thanks for ALL the lessons you have taught me. It has helped me become the Fearless woman I am today.

"We are not on this earth to accumulate victories, things, and experiences, but to be whittled and sandpapered until what's left is who we truly are. This is the only journey that can get us to fearlessness."

Arianna Huffington, author of *On Becoming Fearless...in Love, Work, and Life*

Notes

INTRODUCTION

This book is the journey of self-discovery that led me into the jungle of my own life. My work on being fearless, getting fearless, and staying fearless is intimately tied up with that. The jungle motif seemed appropriate for the journey because most people find themselves lost in the jungle of their minds, and are thrashing about trying to make sense of it. Life is challenging, and there is no easy route to change. You have to do the work you need to do. You have to take the journey through the discomfort and pain, until you reach your safe haven. Until you find yourself.

But where did it all begin? I was born in Leith, Scotland, the port of Edinburgh, which is famous for its annual performing arts festival. Leith is also famous for its whiskey distilleries and is a major shipping center. My father was a dockworker and my mother put labels on whiskey bottles. My father was a raging alcoholic and a violent man. We suffered his rage growing up; he physically abused all of us. My mother's life was a tragic wasteland before she married my father. She had two children, one of whom died, the second survived, but she chose not to live with her. It is believed she was raped but it was never spoken about in the family, so we don't know this for a fact. The message that was hammered into me was never to come home pregnant. If I did, I would be thrown out.

In her third pregnancy with my father, my mother tried to give herself an abortion until she was five months pregnant. Father said he would kill himself if there were more children. The child was born severely retarded. At seven, I became his caretaker because my mother went to work to help feed us. We grew up knowing chaos, rage, violence, and mental abuse and I was raised to believe I would never amount to much. My behavior mirrored that prediction. At sixteen I left home, was busted for drugs shortly after, left for London at seventeen, and was pregnant with my first child at nineteen. In all of this, I did not go home. After being with my child for three months, I placed her up for adoption because I could not imagine raising her to be another me. I wrote about this in my book, *When The Crow Sings*.

I married the first man who cared for me, and I divorced him six years later—leaving him with our son, who was then three. I set out across the Atlantic to live in California en route to Australia, but didn't get that far. In San Francisco, I met my current husband of twenty-nine years. We had two children together, and I adopted his daughter as mine when she was ten, a complete stranger who arrived from Thailand a very frightened child. Through the years, I struggled to find my place as a mother, a wife, and a creative individual without running away.

What follows is the journey I have made to find and reinvent myself, and what I have learned along the way. I wrote this book primarily for women because I have met many who were unsure of their direction, their passion, or their skills and talents, and needed guidance, but the issues contained within apply equally to men. We all have fears, doubts and insecurities. How we choose to handle them is what makes the difference.

If I have learned one thing in life, it is that guides are a necessary part of making it through the confusion and challenge of the jungle landscape. I have had my fair share of them over the last thirty years. As a motivational speaker, my passion is celebrating the journey of each person as she defines and achieves her truest self. At times, it may seem that I am preaching to the choir, in which case I beg your patience with my enthusiasm.

The principles contained here are applicable no matter how old you are. My tag line for being Fearless in my Fifties is: "It's not about Age....it's about Att!tude." I firmly believe the attitude we hold about ourselves is the same attitude that will help us find our way through the jungle of life. It is the confidence that comes from self-knowledge and the willingness to do something different. That att!tude allows you to see the myriad opportunities available and helps you make use of them to further your own path toward becoming the woman you were meant to be.

I am first and foremost a seeker of life, and in order to do that, I frequently step into places that are challenging and have many times over learned to confront my fears. It has been my life's purpose to understand who and what I am, and in doing so, I have discovered I'm not much different from you, nor you from me. We are all in search of something, all living the human experience. Everyone has a personal jungle to pass through. Standing at the edge, you feel full of trepidation and fear, while a small voice inside says, "Go ahead. You can do this." But you hold back because you have heard all the stories of jungle dangers and certain perils waiting there. You don't know what to expect; you feel safer where you are.

But are you?

When you deny the adventure because you feel incapable, unworthy, insecure, anxious, and afraid, you deny the experience of your full potential. You deny the full extent of who you are to become. I have been in that place many times, and each time, I've had to take the first step toward believing I could do it differently. I could become the person I wanted to be, by walking through the jungle of change and reaching the other side. This is the lesson that awaits you.

We all face the same menu of insecurities, the burden of stories held too long in your mind, the nagging issues that hinder your success. You fear insecurity, abandonment, rejection, humiliation, loss, shame, and you suffer guilt because you believe it makes you feel better. You worry, often focusing on things that belong in the realm of your imagination. But the imagination is also where your power center lies. It is the place you can dream, where you can escape the challenges you confront, and where your future begins.

If you can imagine the worst, you can also imagine the best. It's your choice. Whatever you imagine can and will be brought forward into your consciousness if you desire it enough and take action around that desire. It takes as much energy to think positively as it does to think negatively and both cannot occupy the same space at the same time. Your imagination is the only thing between you and living out the full potential of your life.

When you try to make this journey alone, you are destined to take the long road through the jungle, and will use up more energy than necessary as you try to figure it out. This book will be your companion. It will allow you to step into the jungle of your own mind, and travel the road to your own greatness.

Contained within the book is the roadmap towards change. The signposts leading you towards the life you want to live. The connections you need to put all the parts together and allow you to understand who you really are.

Every person who has ever entered the jungle has felt the trepidation of setting foot into unknown territory. You have chosen the path toward fulfillment of your deepest dreams and desires, and you will find your own way. Included in the book are the Tales from the Trail. Stories of women who went from fearful to fearless, they are meant to inspire you to keep moving on your chosen path.

Notes

PART 1
ENTER THE JUNGLE

Notes

CHAPTER 1
Fear is Optional

ΛΛΛΛΛΛΛΛΛΛΛΛΛΛΛΛΛΛΛΛΛΛΛΛΛΛΛΛΛΛΛΛΛΛΛΛΛΛΛΛΛΛΛΛΛΛΛΛΛ

The Bible contains the directive "Do not fear" over two hundred times. The Torah's most repeated commandment is al tirah, "Be not afraid." The Big Book of Alcoholics Anonymous calls fear "An evil and corroding thread" that weaves its way through our lives.

But fear is one of the most powerful motivating forces in the human experience. It is the clarion call; it signals that there is something you need to change in order to live a completely fulfilled life. Honoring this feeling is the greatest gift you can give yourself.

What is Fear?

Fear: A distressing emotion aroused by impending danger, evil, pain, etc., whether the threat is real or imagined; to regard with distrust; doubt and uneasiness. To shrink from doing. To paraphrase Shakespeare - Wherefore art thou fear. Hiding in the bosom of mine heart.

Fear is one of the strongest words in the human emotional language. We would rather say we are anxious, worried or nervous, than say outright we are afraid. Somehow the word *fear* connotes weakness or intense vulnerability so we prefer to cloak it in ambiguous language like "I don't feel like it," "It doesn't work for me", or "I'm too busy, too tired, or too stressed." Fear leads to anger, inappropriate behavior, offensive language or complete rejection. We find tons of excuses to avoid 'feeling' the fear because we all know that fear is alarming, abrasive, unpleasant and painful.

Susan Jeffers in her book *Feel the Fear and Do It Anyway*® says "fear is essentially a lack of belief in your ability to handle whatever comes your way." It is a fundamental lack of trust in you.

But fear is also a basic fact of nature. Whenever you enter unfamiliar territory, you experience it. That vast unknown is where you choose not to go, because you have no idea what is waiting for you, or you can't stand the place between knowing and not knowing. Fear is the abyss of uncertainty that draws you away from making decisions that influence your life in a positive manner; it undermines who you want to be.

Why Do We Ignore It?

Fear is both instinctual and lifesaving. When kept in its rightful place, fear can actually be a vital part of the human experience. In the case of an imminent attack, fear is your body's alarm telling you, "There is danger here. Hide. Run. Fight back. Get help." The action needed is decided by a quick evaluation of the circumstances.

Instantly, when the fear alarm rings, your body prepares for the fight-or-flight reaction. Blood immediately rushes to the core of your body, which is ready to dedicate its energy to the large muscles, leaving your hands and feet cold. Your heart pounds more quickly, in preparation for physical exertion. Adrenaline courses through your body to provide a jolt of needed energy. Digestion shuts down and your body empties itself so you can run faster. Your mind drops its focus on any other activity to keep your attention directly on the matter at hand. This all makes perfect sense if you need to fight off an attack or flee from an enemy but most of the time, it's your imagination on overtime that's causing this reaction.

In this scenario, your body is efficiently launching into its *fight-or-flight* reaction. Each aspect of this physiological event has its basis in preparing your body for combat or the quickest escape route. This reaction may be valuable to people actually encountering savage animals in the jungle. In daily life, however, this magical trick doesn't really help much.

For many people, fear has a warped place of prominence in their lives. In order to meet life's demands and leap into your greatest dreams, you need to learn the real purpose of fear, where it has gone awry in your life, and how you can direct it toward your future success.

Where in YOUR Life Do You Experience Fear?

Regrettably, fear does not just strike when there is something life threatening, it can happen when entering a job interview or starting a new relationship. There are also innumerable versions of intense fear attached to specific experiences—phobias of certain things, such as spiders, airplanes, dogs, and public speaking. Phobic reactions put your mind on steroids, exaggerating the physical reaction to extraordinary heights. At any given moment this can be alarming, embarrassing, and absolutely crippling.

If you have too much fear stimulus, or if your life is filled with dangerous situations, the alarm goes haywire. It may sound constantly, or it might go off intermittently and at inappropriate times. One tragic aspect of a broken danger alarm is that it may not go off when it should. What if your home's fire alarm ignored smoke and flame, but rang wildly whenever you started the dishwasher? Many people live with internal alarms that are just as broken. But eventually, you can also reach a place where the alarm bells are no longer ringing. Fear has simply become a constant part of your life. It holds you in it's grip, confining you to a life of limitation, of uncertainty and certain unhappiness.

Everyone knows people who enter one dangerous situation after another, taking little notice of the hideous consequences coming their way. They don't recognize obvious danger, but are terrified of everyday situations that develop into phobias. Perhaps you let fear stop you from applying for a new job— yet you don't register any fear when driving without your seatbelt, applying for another credit card, or giving an abusive husband one more chance.

Fear helps us to avoid suffering. If you feel afraid when you walk near the edge of a cliff, perhaps you will instead stay a safe distance back from the precipice. If fear strikes when you feel a fire's heat, you will position yourself away from the flames. Applying this to social situations, if someone important in your life has shamed you, you may avoid their friendship. If you were abused in any way, you learn not to trust. No one wants pain, discomfort, embarrassment, humiliation, or rejection, so in order to avoid the consequences, you create all kinds of reasons in your mind why you can't go into a particular situation.

These reasons are the stories people tell themselves. They are the stories inherited from your parents or other significant people in your life. They are the stories you told yourself in order to avoid being hurt and disappointed. They are the stories that no longer serve you. They are the habits you have created in your life.

Learning how to handle your fear, self-doubt and anxiety is what this book is all about. It's about the choices we make when fear shows up in our lives, and ways in which we can minimize our conditioned reaction to these uncomfortable feelings that signal our need to run, defend, react and destroy in order to avoid them. We learn to overcome fear not by running away, but by standing our ground, being willing to make changes in our life, and building confidence by practicing new survival skills over and over again. Fear is an extraordinary motivating force because it sets us a challenge to change something that's not working.

"You gain strength, courage, and confidence by every experience in which you really stop to look fear in the face....You must do the thing which you think you cannot do."—Eleanor Roosevelt

For most people, fear starts in the birth canal. There is a primitive force at work here, and the mother and the child in her womb share emotions equally. The struggle to give birth is one of the most violent acts in the human experience and it is created by nature. Women enter the experience with a great deal of fear because they have heard how painful it will be, and they worry that they are unprepared. They fear for the life of their child and pray that it will be born with all the right body parts and come through this ordeal unscathed. Even today, death can be a major consideration. Generations of this conditioning have been passed down from mother to mother, through fear-filled stories.

A recent article in *The New York Times Magazine* analyzed at length whether fetuses can feel pain. After several experiments (let's not even go there!), it was suggested they can, and it is now standard practice for doctors to anesthetize babies in utero if there is any surgery to be performed. So if they can feel pain, do they also feel fear?

Humans are exquisite creatures whose potential receptivity to all forms of energy is highly developed. If you can feel physical pain, you can also feel emotional pain, no matter how young. During the birthing process, the mother's body contracts in waves of tension as the child pushes its way downwards from the seclusion and security of her watery existence. The child can hear sounds, even if it may not know what they are. It can feel the tightening and the terror as a woman pushes with all her might. With the last push of the head through the bulging vagina, the child is brought into a blinding, light-filled existence of crashing sounds, yelling people, and hands that wrap themselves around her. There is a sudden feeling of being exposed, vulnerable, and yes, afraid. Is it any wonder the child cries when it emerges? Does it want to return to the safety of the womb? The brain may not be able to express that thought, but the whole body reacts instinctively to that need.

After the birth experience is over, fear is quickly forgotten. The trauma of birth is met with a rush of love, warmth, and caring; babies are cherished for being in the lives of their parents.

Fear is like that. Once we are on the other side of whatever it is that was feared, it is quickly forgotten. We frequently say aloud, "What was I so worried about?" Our memories are selective. We remember only that which we need for our survival, until the next time something comes up that jogs the memory and brings us back to a frightening experience.

We live our lives in the past, afraid for the future, unable to connect to the present.

Tales From The Trail
"It's Julie"—Cindy Coughenour

My mission to live *Fearless and Female* began in my teens. It would be a long, sad journey from a playful childhood to tears, fear, personal healing, and eventually finding the power to honor a friend whose journey ended too soon.

It was the summer after my freshman year in college. I was loving life. I was a cheerleader at Wichita State University, a sorority girl, and a member of the WSU Gymnastic team. How could life get any better than this? Too soon, I found out how tragically everything can change in one instant.

I was standing in my parent's kitchen when I heard the reporter on the radio break for a local news story. The words I heard changed my life forever: ***"A nineteen- year-old coed was found murdered in the basement of Brennan Hall, a dormitory at Wichita State University."*** My stomach turned, while my mind raced a thousand miles a minute. I was nineteen and went to Wichita State—I probably had classes with this poor girl. As I stood there in a state of disbelief, the doorbell rang. My dad could see I was in no condition to answer it so he went to see who was intruding on us at this surreal moment. I had always heard the expression *white as a sheet*, but I couldn't imagine what that really looked like. When my father walked back into the kitchen, nothing else could describe the way he looked. The words he spoke stung my ears.

"It's Julie."

The next sound I heard was my own voice screaming.

Julie Marie Ladd had been my next-door neighbor since first grade. As little girls we wore out a path in the grass from her front door to mine. Julie and I played dress-up in petticoats and high heels, strutting up and down the sidewalk almost every day. There were endless games of kickball in our neighborhood and Julie made sure that we reported home as soon as the streetlights came on. I had always been the more daring, tomboy type and Julie the gentler, more mature child. As teens, we spent hours talking about the cute guys her older brother hung out with. After high school, we both enrolled in college at WSU where Julie decided to stretch her wings and try living on campus in an all-women's dormitory. I was busy with sports, school, and the sorority life, while Julie was looking forward to beginning the nursing program at school. Julie and her boyfriend had recently become engaged so they were spending many hours window-shopping for the perfect ring. We were two young women, full of life and hope for the future. Not a worry in the world, until that morning, May 15, 1977.

After Julie's murder, I became obsessed with the fear of being attacked and murdered. I also struggled with the question of why. Why did this happen? Why Julie? She didn't have a mean bone in her body. I thought of her last minutes so often and I played them over and over again in my mind. I used to stand outside of Julie's dormitory and picture her walking to class with a smile that melted the hearts of men, and her genuine sweet spirit that welcomed women to be her friend.

But the fear I felt was the worst. I would mentally place myself in the last few minutes of Julie's life over and over again. What would I have done? Would I scream? fight? cry and plead for my life? It was paralyzing to realize that I had *no* idea how to physically defend myself in that type of situation. I was afraid to leave the house and go to school. If I did go to school, I was afraid to come home to an empty house. In the mornings, I couldn't stay in the house alone. I had to have my dad wait until I got out of the shower, dressed, keys in hand, and then we walked out to our cars together. I saw no end to this feeling of helplessness.

One day, my very wise mother sat me down and said, "You may never get the answer to *why*. Maybe you should search for the *what*. What can you do to honor Julie's life because you aren't honoring her by sitting at home being afraid." At that moment the direction of my life began to change. I didn't know it, but it was happening. First, I decided to face what I was really afraid of. I realized that I was terrified of being physically attacked. As children, Julie and I learned how to dance, swim, and drive a car, but we had never been taught how to protect our bodies if we were physically attacked. So, I started getting in touch with friends from college who had gone into law enforcement and asked them to teach me self-defense. I read everything I could get my hands on about personal safety, and I'm sure I bored many a friend with my endless re-enactments of the perfect palm-heel strike to the nose and a feisty knee to the groin. At first it was just a matter of learning how to physically protect myself, but as my training continued, I could also feel how strong and empowered my mind was becoming. Little by little, the day-to-day paralyzing fear was fading and a strong FEARLESS woman was emerging. I knew this training was very healing for me, but I still had the pain in my heart of losing my friend and not knowing how to keep her memory alive.

As the years passed, I continued to train, and one day a friend asked me to speak at her church and teach women these life-saving skills. What was she thinking? I'm not a professional, who would listen to me? Before I could say, "Thanks, but I don't think so," I heard myself say, "I'd love to!" That night, as I was preparing notes for my upcoming program, it all became so clear. This is the way I can honor Julie's life.

Standing behind the podium, at my very first speaking engagement, I could feel my knees shaking. But as I looked out into the audience, I could see Julie and myself in the faces of these women and young girls. I could see the young carefree girls that we once were, and I could picture us as the strong, older women that we both could have become. The strength to speak that day came from deep inside my soul. I was teaching these women the things that Julie and I should have been taught when we were young women. At that moment, the fear of so many years left my body.

I now travel the country speaking to women and teens, teaching them skills of survival. I love standing behind the bag watching their faces as they hit, punch, and kick. I get to see the moment that fear abandons their body and they realize they can fight back. Every time I speak to groups of women, I share Julie's story. These lucky women are now learning to live their safest lives possible because of my dear friend Julie Marie Ladd.

"Everyone has talent. What is rare is the courage to follow the talent to the dark place where it leads."—Erica Jong

Stepping into the Jungle

Ask yourself:

What fears are holding you back? Are these fears real or imagined?

What would you have done differently, if fear had not gotten in the way?

Where in life do you hide your fear by filling my time with busyness, distractions or pushing the emotion away?

Finish the phrase: Because of fear, I abandoned my dreams of becoming…

What would it look like if you could remove fear from my life? What benefits do you think you would gain?

If you were to trust that you could be fearless, what would that look like?

CHAPTER 2
Be Willing to Change

▲▲

"People cannot discover new lands until they have the courage to lose sight of the shore."—Andre Gide

When we launch the boat, there is no telling where we will end up. Christopher Columbus thought he was going to India!

How Much Pain Are You In?

Early in my journey to develop a healthy attitude to life, I was greatly influenced by the works of Clarissa Pinkola Estes, noted psychologist and the author of *Women Who Run With the Wolves*. For the first time, I was presented with the idea that we choose our parents. At that time, I wondered how that could possibly be true. Why would I choose to come into a family that was completely chaotic, violent, and abusive? Many of you reading this will be thinking, "that's nuts! No one would choose what I had to go through." In my case, it took me a while to sit with that idea before I finally understood that life is about making choices, so why wouldn't I choose my parents. There were certain life lessons to be learned, and while it could be seen as harsh, the evolution of my character was strengthened by what I endured in my early days. My mind was a generational tar pit of anger, self-hate, depression, sadness, and grief. Oh, yes, we do inherit the sins of the fathers and the mothers. I grew up with chaos so I learned to recreate it in my own life.

But as my journey continued, I began to see the lessons to be learned. I believe that the main purpose of life is to learn who you are, how your world functions, and what is your place in it. So why wouldn't you choose parents from whom you could learn some of life's greatest lessons? In my case, I had to learn compassion, forgiveness, and self-esteem. I've learned how to overcome great odds, using my intelligence, humor, determination, strength, indomitable spirit, and wonderful creativity to move beyond the circumstances of my birth and environment. I have learned to ask for MORE—and received it.

"I find that it is not the circumstances in which we are placed, but the spirit in which we face them, that constitutes our comfort."—
Elizabeth T. King

What Are You Willing to Give Up?

Change usually means we have to sacrifice something. Whether it's a bad relationship, a job that no longer satisfies, an abusive habit, or an unhealthy approach to our body. What usually kicks in is what I call *the deprivation syndrome*. That sense of loss and deprivation that comes when you make changes in your life, even if those changes are moving you in the direction of positive self-growth. You see we are habituated to our negativity, addicted to the effects of it.

Fear is a learned response. We are conditioned into it so we can be conditioned out of it.

In 1920, Dr. John B. Watson performed a psychological experiment on a nine-month-old child, training him to be afraid of furry white objects. Little Albert, was presented with various objects he was not afraid of and his responses were recorded. Later, he was presented with these objects again, only this time some of them were accompanied by a loud sound that frightened the boy. Eventually, Dr. Watson's work led the boy toward a fear of rats, Santa Claus, and a man with white hair (presumably the doctor). John Watson was also a proponent of rigid training for children, including toilet training from three months and limiting physical touch from children. Today, you might say that Watson was psychotic, but he was one of the most revered child psychologists of his day.

Benjamin Spock, a former acolyte of Watson, was one of the first to refute his methodology, creating his own approach to child rearing. My generation raised our children on Spock because it was a much more lenient and liberating experience for parents and children, but eventually his methodology has also been questioned.

There is no such thing as perfect child rearing. D.W. Winnicott, a noted child psychologist, gave the best blessing of all to parenting when he wrote in the 1950s about *The Good Enough Mother*. This provided the greatest relief to me as I struggled to find my place as a mother to my children. More than any other aspect of my existence, learning how to become *a good enough mother* has been my journey.

As anyone growing up in an abusive home knows firsthand, when Father is a violent drunk, children learn to run for cover at the sound of the door opening. My brother and I used to hide under the table. Some children wet their pants at the sound of an angry voice, so deep is their fear reaction. I wet the bed until I was nine years old. I used to duck every time someone raised his or her hand quickly, even into my thirties. Having grown up in poverty, money discussions can make a grown woman's stomach turn flips for fear of financial insecurity. In my household growing up, I watched my mother's despair on a daily basis. These are all conditioned responses to negative behavior, which I adopted as my own until much later in life.

What is Your Commitment to Change?

Taking an honest look at your life, you can see that your choices have been influenced by fear much more often than ambition for good results or your true desires. In fact, when analyzing your own life, you may see a pattern of fear that will amaze you. My clients insist that uncovering this pattern is essential to changing their ways. As one client told me recently, "I'm afraid to really be who I want to be because I will hurt someone, or fail them in some way. I say yes when I mean no, and I get so mad at myself and hate them for putting me in this place. I know that all I need to do is stop considering them first, and put me up there, but it's hard."

It *is* hard, but you must start to put yourself first. Making that commitment to change what isn't working is the greatest gift you can give yourself. By learning how to love yourself, you allow others to love you more and allow them to figure things out for themselves. You can't fix anyone, nor should you try. It's hard enough changing yourself, without trying to change or fix someone else. When I eventually woke up to the fact that anything that went wrong in my very long marriage was not always my fault, I felt very liberated. I reached a place where I could say to my husband with absolute conviction, "This is not about me, this is about you," and he would accept that possibility.

As long as you make yourself the culprit, you are not showing self-love and you are not allowing the other person to take responsibility for their part in the drama.

Each one of us carries the innate and valuable fear that is standard to our humanness. Throw a baby up in the air and you will get what is called 'the startle reflex'. It may not understand that you may drop it, but it understands that it is now in an unsafe position with nothing between it and the air around it. My youngest daughter used to have a game when she was about nine months old. She would scurry to the bottom of our bed and launch herself off the end knowing we would catch her ankles before she fell headlong onto the floor. If she had hit the floor a few times, it's a good bet that she would have given that game up. She would have internalized the pain as fear and used it to keep herself safe.

But there is yet another aspect of fear, and it is the most paralyzing of all. Many are committed to a fear of personal growth and change. In his book, *A Psychology of Being*, this is what Abraham Maslow described as "the struggle against our own greatness."

How many people struggle with proving who they are? They underplay, undermine, and underwhelm, not only themselves but also the people they meet in life. They cover up their

41

life with facades. The successful businesswoman, the doting mother, the dutiful daughter, the good wife, the helpful friend...but underneath these roles, there may be quite a different feeling. Being honest with yourself about who you are and what you want means stepping up to your greatness. But that's where many fail. They play small when they want to play big. They allow others to think less of them because they don't step forward into being the best they can be.

When you play small by keeping yourself modest, humble, accommodating, and soft-spoken, you are denying the world your presence, but more importantly, you are living your life from a half-self-life perspective instead of embracing your whole self. Your capacity to be great is confined by your ability to step forward and truly declare who you are without the fear that you will be found to be a fraud. Unfortunately, many feel that way, including some highly successful people.

Everyone has secret selves, thoughts, and desires they don't want people to find out about. We hide negative thoughts that minimize who we are. "I'm really not very smart, so I won't bother raising my hand" or "they'll find out that I'm just faking it." Both are places of judgment and both are predicated upon rejection or abandonment. Most of the times a person refuses to step into their greatness, it is for that reason, and none other.

When making change you must move beyond the place known as the comfort zone. But because you fear that many of the myths and beliefs you have about yourself may actually be true, you don't try, so therefore, you can't fail. For every minute you invest in preserving the status quo, you further avoid the possibility of failure.

But if you are to live a fulfilling life, you have to learn how to step into your greatness, get past your fears, and find a better way of living without the feelings, thoughts, and learned behaviors that crippled you.

"Your playing small doesn't serve the world. There's nothing enlightened about shrinking so that other people won't feel insecure around you. We are all meant to shine, as children do."—Marianne Williamson

Tales From The Trail
"Like a Virgin"—Janet Andrew

In a recent commencement speech, First Lady Michelle Obama shared what it is like to be the first generation in her family to go to college. As I read her valedictorian speech to the graduating class at UC-Merced, I remembered the fears I had to face in high school in Detroit on whether I would be good enough to be the first in my family to graduate from college. But I also remembered the reason why so many didn't make it that far.

My parents were the children of farmers and because there was no money for higher education they both worked in the auto factories, along with most of their siblings. The two handsome older brothers who were my heroes and protectors ended up joining the armed forces—the younger of the brothers first finished an associate degree at a community college and then trained as a helicopter pilot in the Army and fought in Vietnam. Both successfully pursued technical trades and raised families. I was the only one who was both determined and successful in my efforts to get a four year degree. My father fueled the dream, excited that one of his kids might become a teacher; his own thwarted passion. My mother just wanted me to get safely married.

All through high school, I was the nerd who spent most of my time studying. So it was no surprise that at the completion of my senior year, my friends and family encouraged me to start dating. It wasn't the easiest of things for me. In truth, I was mortally shy and I didn't have a date for my senior prom. Most of my classmates in my honors high school program came from middle and upper class families with money for overseas vacations and clothes I could only dream about. I was hopelessly out of fashion and just threw myself into my love of art, music and books. I hung out with friends from my working class neighborhood and with cousins in my large extended family.

My angst over my lack of social skills paled next to my bliss that summer at the prospect of starting college in the fall at Wayne State University (WSU) in downtown Detroit. But as the summer progressed, my mother worried about my seeming lack of interest in men, although she also declared a 10PM curfew because, as she later told me, she wanted to protect my virginity and save me the pain she experienced in an unhappy first "shotgun" marriage. I secretly thanked her for the support, although I realize now that I never openly acknowledged that an early curfew turned out to be a blessing. Nor did I confide to my family how terrified I was.

I met Jack later that summer on a blind double date with a neighborhood girlfriend. I was intrigued by Alice, who was smart, flirty, bold and uninterested in college and had a full-time summer job selling cosmetics. I was tongue-tied and worked part-time selling books at the downtown Hudson's department store. Jack and his friend were in college upstate and looking for summer fun.

The glamour of dating a handsome, brown-eyed frat guy appealed to me, but I also worried that I was in over my head. How could I get through college if I got pregnant and got married? I was so naïve I wasn't even certain how women could get pregnant or how I could prevent it. Birth control was a forbidden subject. One night as I lay in bed, I came up with a solution—I would wear my panty girdle on all of our dates, just in case he got that far. I was sure it would get me through the summer. It would be my chastity belt.

I underestimated Jack's tenacity. After a month of innocent dates, he and his friend took Alice and I to a buddy's apartment. We sat laughing and drinking beer in the small living room until long after 9PM. With no drinking experience, I got an almost instant high. Soon, Alice and her date disappeared to get more beer and chips while Jack and I sat on the couch. His kisses became insistent, alternating with professions of love. He wanted to marry me. Jack quickly had me pinned under him and I started to cry. "We have to go," I pleaded. "I have a curfew."

"Ok, next time," he said urgently, demanding that I agree.

"Yes, next time," I said, afraid to make him angry, and relieved as the other couple walked back into the room.

As we drove home, I was ashamed that I had not seen the limitations of a panty girdle—it couldn't speak back—and it had not stopped me from promising him my virginity so easily. A few days later I found the courage to pick up the phone and tell Jack goodbye. I didn't fully realize it then, but this was a turning point in my life, a critical moment for my future. Had I succumbed to Jack's (and partially my own) desires, my life could have turned out entirely different.

Jack wasn't giving up easily. He showed up pleading at my front door the next weekend. I stayed resolute and turned him away, telling my puzzled parents I wasn't interested in him. That wasn't completely true. I knew so little about Jack, his real dreams, whether we had anything in common besides our passion, not sure if he read the kind of poetry and literature I adored. I was so attracted to him and so confused by his behavior.

Just a few weeks later, and when so many young girls succumb to the promises of love during the summer, I successfully started college as a virgin. I avoided dating during freshman year, and instead rejoiced in finding new friends of both sexes with the same passion for learning that I had. I found my true soul mates on the campus newspaper and was soon volunteering, first as a photographer, then as a reporter. I had given myself the time to find my calling as a writer and journalist.

By my junior year in college, the women's movement was underway, abortion was being legalized with Roe vs. Wade, and the pill was new on the market. For the first time, it seemed that women from all backgrounds had more options for controlling their destiny. Today, even as more second generation Americans break through barriers that held their parents back from higher education, too many teenagers in poor communities still have a hard time breaking out of the 'family traditions,' including teen pregnancy, that keep them from pursuing their dreams.

I am deeply grateful that I found the courage, with the help of my parents, to overcome my obstacles and pursue my degree and discover the career in journalism and public relations that I love and that ultimately made my family so proud of me.

Stepping into the Jungle

Ask yourself:

Where in your family life did you learn not to trust? What messages did you receive growing up?

Where in your life do you not trust yourself? Does it stop you from achieving all the success you want in your relationships, career, creativity, etc.

What negative thoughts are you holding that keep you in limitation?

What do you get from refusing to change? What is your investment in staying 'stuck'?

What are you willing to give up to create a better life for yourself?

What would make it easier for you to commit to change right now? Do you need support, are you willing to take the risk involved in doing something different?

What direction do you want to take that would help you live a more positive, nurturing life than the one you're presently living?

Notes

CHAPTER 3
Know Your Outcome

ᚠᚠ

"What lies behind us and what lies before us are tiny matters compared to what lies within us."—Oliver Wendell Homes

You are much stronger than you think, and much more capable than you give yourself credit for. Tap into the power that is within you.

Where Do You Want to Go?

Four women stroll along a paved walking path and notice a shaded, winding trail leading into a dark and mysterious jungle. A hand-painted sign at the entrance promises the adventure of a lifetime, untold treasures, and true, lasting happiness to anyone who dares set foot upon this trail and follow it through the entire jungle. The four women discuss among themselves the wild creatures, frightening situations, and treacherous terrain awaiting any who travel that route. Three of the women, determined to change the course of their lives and fully realize their dreams, decide to enter that jungle, despite grave danger and certain difficulty.

Now, how many women are left standing on the paved path, gazing into the darkened jungle with trepidation?

Four.

You see, the three brave ones *decided* to enter. And that is as far as many people take it. Everyone has experienced good intentions. It manifests in your desire to go to the gym regularly, eat the right kinds of food, get more sleep, work less, spend more time with your children. But it is not a real decision until you are ready to commit to the action that follows. You must take the first baby step toward changing the program of your life, even if you are scared to death.

You are at the entrance of that rugged trail right now. But all the deciding in the world isn't going to take you to a new place until you take the first step. If you are ready, you will enter this jungle and experience the rich colors, scents, and music all around you. Putting one foot in front of the other, taking risks with enthusiasm, facing the truth in your heart, you can turn that decision into results. You will know the exhilarating thrill of pushing yourself to new limits, and you will reach a place in which you are able to lead other women on the same journey.

When you take a decision you are making a commitment to change what isn't working. You are ready to step up to the challenge and create something different for you that will lead you towards living your best life now. But if there's one thing I've learned along the way it's this. You have to start with the end in mind. Stephen Covey in his book *The 7 Habits of Highly Effective People* wrote that you cannot get from dependence (caught up in your negative behavior) to independence (creating the life you truly want to live) without having a vision of where it is you are going.

Before you begin your journey through the jungle, you must first know what it is you seek. If you begin with this vision in your mind, you will then be able to create it in your world.

So ask yourself, where do you want to go? What do you want to achieve? What would make you happy? What would make you feel like you're truly living your best life now? What will that look like when you get there?

Often, we stagger through our lives much like a pinball machine hoping that balls will hit the holes with the biggest dividends. Random acts, random thoughts, random direction. But when we can get specific about what our future looks like, it is remarkable the success we can achieve.

What Do You Want To Achieve?

When I started my business I knew only one thing. I wanted to send a message to as many people as I could about how to get beyond the fears, doubts and anxieties that stop you from living up to your true potential. I had no idea what it would take for me to achieve this goal, but I was willing to step outside my comfort zone to find out. Fueled by a vision of what I wanted, I set forth on my epic journey through the jungle of my life. Now, this may sound dramatic, but let's face it, dealing with the twists and turns of our internal landscape can feel like an epic journey, and many of you reading this are thinking, I'm not on an epic journey. I'm not even sure I want to be on the path at all. It sounds like it's too much hard work but hey, I'm interested enough to check it out. Part of the reason you're reading this is to find some solutions to getting yourself out of wherever you are now, into whatever it is you hope to achieve. But you may not know what that looks like, yet. At present, you're staring down the path, wondering what awaits you now that you've made a commitment to change. Life is about risk, and as I like to say Respect your Intention and Show Kourage. R.I.S.K.

"Without intention any hope is stillborn. With intention you have only to put your foot in the river and there is no telling the seas you will see, the transformations you will experience."—Noah Ben Shea

What Will Your Plan Look Like?

Do you want to be a better mother, as I did? Or would you like to become a recognized expert in your field? Maybe you would like to be an artist, writer, singer or other creative person. It doesn't matter what it is. If it's something that is beyond where you are now you need to be specific about that that looks like. Until we create a specific picture of what our soul is searching for, and start to take action towards it by writing it down, it is a stillborn decision.

So let's look at what you need to do to make your dreams a reality.

Start with a blank notebook. There are several elements to building a profile of your goal. You need to know:

◊ What is it?

◊ How long will it take me to get there?

◊ What do I need to do to make it happen?

◊ What will be the results when I achieve it.

◊ Remember, start with the end in mind.

First, defining your goals is critical. If you don't know what they are, then think about what turns you on? What sets you on fire and makes you want to get out of bed in the morning? What is it that if you didn't do it, your life would never feel fulfilled? Let there be no limit to your imagination.

If you can't define that, then do some brainstorming around the things that give you pleasure in life and see if you can't find some common threads. That's the point of departure for your journey into the jungle.

Look at the following points.

◊   Career

◊   Relationships

◊   Fun

◊   Achievements

◊   Money

◊   Possessions

Each one of them is a part of your life.

Question every aspect of your goals. Take your time, as you don't want to end up with wishy-washy goals you probably won't even relate to a month later.

Take six pieces of paper—one for each the six areas mentioned above, and brainstorm over each for at least three minutes. Write down what you would like to have, achieve, and do in each area.

Secondly, how long do you need to accomplish your goals? When would you like to see it manifest by? Setting a deadline is critical. If you don't have a definite date in mind, then you can't possibly have anything to shoot for. Not only should you be setting goals that are time defined, but they should also be quantified as well. The more specific you are with your goals, the easier it will be to reach them.

Write down on each category the approximate timescale within which you want to realistically achieve your goals. Categorize the goals into the following timescale categories:

◊   Less than 1 year

◊   1–3 years

◊   3 years plus

You now have six lists of things you would like to achieve and the time frame within which you wish to achieve them. Read them through carefully.

Take from each area, those goals for which you have allotted less than 1 year and select the top two from each section.

This leaves you with 12 goals achievable within one year.

If you have any "I should" on your goal list turn all your "I should do this" goals to "I must DO this" goals.

Ask yourself what is the goal is and why you feel you *must* achieve it. Then ask yourself the following questions.

◊   *What pleasure will it give you?*

◊   *What will you be able to do?*

◊ *What will you miss out on if you don't achieve it?*

◊ *Why is it so important to you?*

◊ *Why is the goal a MUST rather than a SHOULD?*

We are talking about motivation here, and to be motivated must be a burning desire to achieve something.

Tales From The Trail
"My Turning Point"—Lynn Scheurell

Everyone has a turning point but we don't always recognize it until we've reached the other side.

It was 1997, and I had taken a job with a consulting firm in Chicago two months earlier. My supervisor had taken me under his wing, and I was adjusting to the job when I received an offer to work at a start-up .com in Salt Lake City, Utah. I wasn't even unpacked from my first move, and here I was packing up and moving again. I'd never been to Utah, so I had no idea where I was going. It was the other side of the world and I had no one to help me get set up. I rented an apartment—sight unseen—over the internet, and drove for three days cross-country (hauling my car behind me).

On the way, I called my new colleagues to ask for help and, not surprisingly, no one was available. I wondered if I had made the right choice, but after all, they didn't know me and unpacking my belongings wasn't their problem or responsibility. Arriving at my new apartment, I found help from two young guys and paid them to help me. I was deeply appreciative. With one day to get myself oriented, feeling completely alone, cut off from support systems nearly 2,000 miles away, reeling from a second huge life change in as many months, not knowing anything about the city, about my job or how things were going to turn out, I walked into the chaos of a start-up internet company. It was beginning to feel like Mr. Toad's Wild Ride and I was scared.

Over the next fifteen months or so, I lived on shifting sand. In retrospect, I don't know how I did it. Not only was I adjusting to a new life (I also had my car broken into—my purse, company laptop, and cash all taken) and feeling the shock of floundering in a Mormon social culture of which I wasn't ever going to be a part. On top of everything else, my job description kept changing. The leader of the .com was a visionary whose creativity went unbounded, so our job responsibilities changed daily. I did everything from customer service to sales presentations to administrative support, and more. It was hard to know where I fit in, and because I'm a generalist, I see the bigger picture. It was chaotic to say the least, but I had the uncanny knack of knowing what needed to be done, and then doing it. For this reason, they came to rely on me but I was a maverick and preferred to do things my own way, which fit well with the constantly changing scenery I was part of. In my role as a professional catalyst who helps small business owners make sense of their needs, that personal asset came in very handy.

The downside of all this shape-shifting was a fair amount of internal completion at the .com. Jockeying for security and internal competition became the name of the game. Since I really didn't know how to play that political game, and didn't know how to play by those unwritten rules, (either then or now), I lost out in the end. I was the first in a long line of lay-offs. This one happened on December 15, 1998—ten days before Christmas—and I had no clue what would happen next. I had never felt so defeated.

For the next three months, I lay on my couch in a deep unrelenting depression, uncertain what to do. I was renting a house from a married (now former) colleague to whom I had a dysfunctional attraction. I had no financial reserves or support and felt betrayed by the company I had worked so hard for. I couldn't bear to think about getting a new job (since I felt that would only set me up for more pain), and I also knew then that I couldn't function with my 'old' way of doing things. Something had to change, but I had no idea what it would be or what it would look like.

I was at a turning point, and I only realize it now, looking back. I HAD to do something different because I didn't want to return to this *dark scary place* ever again, this place where my well being would be dictated and controlled by someone else. My life's energy had gone into building someone else's dream and now all of that had been ultimately devalued. As a result, I had somehow lost a part of myself, and I vowed this would never happen again.

That's when I did the one thing that made me feel right—*I followed the energy.* Over and over, everywhere I went, I'd been seeing references to Feng Shui—a newspaper ad, a billboard, a story on TV. I approached the teacher of a Feng Shui practitioner training course, told her that I needed to take her class but couldn't pay for it, and she let me work the course tuition off in her store. It was the gift that started giving me back my life, the confidence and internal energy I had lost. I re-connected to the one thing that now guides and supports me living every day since—my conscious connection to the *source energy* of Feng Shui.

Only now, more than a decade later, do I fully understand what happened to me at that .com when I lost my job on what felt like the most disastrous day of my life. In that *moment*, when I was overflowing with the fear of not knowing what was next, when I was replete with the oppressive feeling that I had hit bottom in my career and had used up all my resources and wouldn't make it another day… in that *moment* on that disastrous day, I received my greatest gift from the Universe. That was my *turning point*, my chance to get on the right track with living and being and expressing my true purpose in life. And I'm happy to report that my life has been just that ever since.

In closing, here's my advice to anyone feeling the fear of a particular situation: experience it deeply and use it to find your own personal *moment*—your *turning point*. Your life will never be the same.

Stepping into the Jungle

Ask yourself:

What do you want to achieve in your lifetime? What have you desired and not followed through on?

If you achieve your goals, what will this give you? What are the benefits of getting what you want?

What will it take for you to get there? What do you need to do more of, less of, the same?

Where are you willing to take risks? What are you willing to say YES to?

Where in your life do you avoid risks? What are you avoiding when you say NO?

What decision do you need to take today that will start you in the direction you want to go?

CHAPTER 4
Enjoy the Journey

"You have brains in your head. You have feet in your shoes. You can steer yourself any direction you choose. You're on your own. And you know what you know. And YOU are the guy who'll decide where to go. Oh, the Places You'll Go.—Dr. Seuss"

You have traveled far in this lifetime both internally and externally. You have changed so many times without thinking, but you still don't believe you are capable of getting what you want. But you can. You just have to decide.

Do You Think Change Is Easy?

Nobody said change was easy. You are breaking habits that have been acquired over a lifetime of negative conditioning.

When you are lost in the jungle of life, unsure of which way to go or what to bring on the trip, you are living in survival mode, afraid of what comes next. You don't trust that you know what you know, and you fight the branches of your life to clear the way so you can see where you're going, only to find there are more tangles and blockages than before.

The jungle appears vast, and you feel small—but it is only your perception that you are small and lost in a huge place because you cannot know the entire picture from the small space you inhabit at the entrance. You are already in fear of what the jungle holds and you imagine worst-case scenarios. The wild animals of your fear, the insects of insecurity, the twisted paths of misdirection, the broken trail of dreams not met, the landslides blocking healthy relationships—these are the elements of life, and they are all in the jungle of your mind. But if you understand that you cannot KNOW anything beyond where you stand at that moment, then the journey becomes one of discovery as you move from moment to moment.

Few of us care to enter unknown, forbidding territory. You don't know what's waiting for you there. Your mind shifts into overdrive, creating the worst possible scenarios. You stand quivering at the entrance and derive great satisfaction from knowing you are being sensible and can't possibly do what you think you can do. You think it is better just to stay where you are.

But there is another vantage point—one from much further up the trail, looking over your shoulder at those who follow in your footsteps. You are not alone. Women have been doing this for ages. I have done it, and the women who wrote the *Tales from the Trail* have done it.

My family spent many hours hiking through the Rockies and the beautiful State Parks of the Western United States and Canada. Much of it was extremely challenging but we were motivated to get to the top to see the view, all the while climbing upwards with children in tow.

During these hikes, we frequently set out on a trail with only a map, a supply of water and food, and a strong desire to see what we could of this astonishing landscape. Occasionally the trail was tricky enough that we needed a guide to take us through the high passes and confusing waterways. It was sensible because we had no interest in getting lost in the wilderness, although there were times when we did. And there were other times that we wished we had a guide. When it was getting dark, or when the path disappeared and we had to backtrack. It was a little scary at these times, but we always managed to make it back to our car.

Fear has been described as the *sharp edge of excitement* and you are discovering the truth of that. Fear is one of the most powerful motivating forces we have. When you acknowledge that, when you accept the challenge of change, that's when powerful things start to happen. And it all begins with your thinking.

Are You Focused?

The mind is a powerful place. EVERYTHING you are, everything you experience, everything you create in your life, is a product of your mind. The mind is always creating and interpreting. It is conditioned by what you believe. It is your own, personal reality based on these perceptions. This is the territory of the jungle. This is where your biggest fears lie, and your biggest opportunities exist. Learning how to navigate the jungle of your mind is your mission. Keep your eye on the goal and the rest will take care of itself.

You may remember the television show *Mission Impossible*, and the movies starring Tom Cruise. Most of their tasks were indeed impossible at first glance, but the protagonists of the show always managed to find a solution that would retrieve the prize. They put their fine minds to the task and devoted their attention to the solution, not the problem. You may have watched it and said, "Yeah, right," but you had to admire their ingenuity, or sheer dumb luck, in achieving the results.

What the hero's stories all had in common was the ability to fly into the abyss of the unknown. It's what everyone wishes they could do. In your secret place, you dream of being able to scale tall buildings, leap across chasms, and fly above the world unhindered by gravity. You want the excitement of *Mission Impossible*, but not the scary stuff that goes with it. Unfortunately, the scary stuff is part of the ride.

In the desire to manage our fears, we believe if only things were perfect, life would be fine. If only we could control the elements of our lives, we would feel safe. If only we could limit our expectations, we wouldn't ever be disappointed. If we refuse to speak up even when wronged, then we'll be safe. No one will have the opportunity to reject, abandon, or ridicule us. We will be safe if we limit the expression of who we really are. But will we?

When you learn how to confront the obstacles, accept the challenges, and go beyond the barriers of your negativity in your mind, these barriers disappear. The mind does not discriminate. You do. You are the master of your own fate if you wish to be.

From *Mission Impossible* to *The Mission*, (is there a theme here?) Robert de Niro plays a conquistador with a long history of violence and mayhem behind him. He finds God, and in order to repent, he has to climb a mountain to work at a mission high up in Northeastern Argentina called Las Missionas. As part of his self-imposed punishment, he hauls an enormous sack of heavy silver armor up the mountain. Though it nearly kills him, he is determined to pay the price and won't let the weight drop. Eventually, the priest, played by Jeremy Irons, helps him realize he can let it go... drop the whole damn thing over the cliff and move along.

I was like the conquistador. Just as I had suffered the mayhem and chaos of other people's lives, I too left a trail of mayhem and ruined lives behind me in my early years. The wounds of generations are strong and usually keep repeating until someone has the courage to break the cycle. In my early therapy sessions, I was damned if I would give up the wounds easily, and damned because of holding on. Letting go of old wounds, old habits, old behaviors, old truths, sometimes means you have to climb the mountain, or enter the jungle, to let them go.

Everyone has suitcases, trunks, and closets full of stories. You carry this weight to show you have gained experience, can justify why you feel the way you do, and stop yourself from moving forward. It is the baggage of your life.

When you travel in the jungle, everything you have is on your back. Your sleeping arrangements, food, toileting needs, water, clothing, equipment, everything travels with you in a pack. Knowing you are responsible for carrying it the entire trip, you may be surprised at how selective your packing becomes. No one wants to carry more than they need, because an extra few ounces can become unbearable when added to a full pack of essential supplies.

Thinking along these lines, it is easy to see that there is no need to stuff a blow dryer, stiletto heels, or an electric blanket into your backpack, but you often choose to carry emotional baggage that is just as useless and potentially dangerous. You've got to dump the entire contents out on the ground and figure out what you've got in there that doesn't belong. What is weighing you down and paining you over and over again. What are you finally ready to leave behind?

In my own life, I was running scared for my first forty years. I buried my fears in overworking, over-pleasing, over-con-trolling, over-compensating behaviors that left me dried up and exhausted. I was tired of surviving. Tired of waiting to be found out, tired of doubting what I was capable of becoming. Dumping out the contents of my life was a painful process, but I knew if I did not do it, then it would destroy me.

It is the tragedies, disappointments, and struggles that really help you to appreciate the fullness of who you truly are—but only if you are willing to confront and move beyond them. It is important to KNOW THYSELF in order to appreciate the gifts of your life. But sometimes it just feels like too much. Sometimes it seems that living through the difficulty is accomplishment enough; while turning the experience into a positive state of learning is simply too much to ask.

I recently watched the movie *La Vie En Rose* about the singer Edith Piaf, an icon in France. The actress who played her was brilliant, capturing, in a powerful performance, the nuances of a destructive and destroyed personality. But the thing that bothered me about her story was not the repeated tragedies that showed up in her life, but her refusal to get beyond them. To the end she was a narcissistic, destructive human being.

Her tragedies had literally crippled her, because she had severe arthritis from an early age. Her voice was the one gift she could give to the masses, and they devoured her. By the end of the movie, I was disappointed. I felt sorry for the losses she encountered, for the betrayals that surrounded her, for the adoration that indulged her every whim, but in the end, it all meant nothing because she was incapable of overcoming the early tragedies of her life. This was the most profound loss of all.

Who wants to get to the end of their life and ask, "Is that all there is?" Or would you prefer the famous Piaf song *No Regrets*? Wouldn't you rather slide in sideways, with a glass of champagne in your hand, yelling, "Wow! That was a helluva ride."

What Are You Grateful For?

There are myriad ways to distract you from what is important in your life. The lucky ones are those who are jolted awake one day and realize how wrapped up in the negatives they've become; how one corner of their lives has somehow become the focus of their entire life warping their expectations and sense of self-worth.

The changing landscape of your mind, your body and your behavior can cause great unrest in your soul. The ground doesn't feel safe. The elements seem threatening. There are wild beasts lurking in hidden places that threaten your existence. But when you are focused on the negativity in your life created by fear, anxiety and self-doubt, you neglect to see the beauty that exists. Within every jungle there is magnificent beauty. In your life it's called joy, gratitude, serenity, hope, kindness, compassion, forgiveness and love.

All of these are the gifts we get from living our life truly being who we want to be. I believe all human beings are innately kind, considerate and generous. I believe we are conditioned to believe otherwise, and because I am an eternal optimist, I believe we are blessed with gifts we can't even imagine having.

Learning how to be grateful for the small things in life takes awareness. I keep a gratitude journal by my bed, and each night, before I go to sleep, I write for five minutes about the things I appreciated about my day. The people I met, the opportunities that came my way, the events that made a difference. It is a way of programming your brain towards the good stuff.

When we change our thinking, it takes time and it takes a willingness to go the extra distance and notice when things are not in line with your new way of being.

A simple way of doing this is to keep a stack of note cards nearby. Two piles. One for negative thoughts and one for positive thoughts. Write them down when they occur, as near to the time they occurred as possible. State the emotion and state the event that precipitated them. Do this over one week and see how it adds up. My guess is that you will soon see a pattern emerging. You will start to see some of the trigger points that keep you in a downward negative spiral instead of an upward positive one. It may not be as negative as you think. Dr. Barbara Fredrickson wrote in her book *Positivity* that when we are positive it broadens our outlook on life. When you are walking through a jungle, if you keep your eye constantly on the lookout for the dangers, then you will miss the beauty.

You will miss the opportunities to enjoy the scenery because your focus is too narrow. Life is meant to be enjoyed not endured. You always have a choice.

Tales from the Trail
"Lovely Illusion"—Gabrielle Yetter

Everyone thought we were the perfect couple.

We met in a bar in New York while I was traveling around the States with my girlfriend, Wendy, from South Africa. Jeff and I instantly connected. He offered us a place to stay for a few days so we could save money on a hotel.

Wendy and I moved into his spare room and she left soon after to return home. I moved from the spare room into Jeff's room and we were married less than a year later.

He was a number of years older than I and, at the tender age of twenty-five, I found him fascinating. He owned a business, had two wonderful sons (almost my age), was successful and popular, and wanted to share his life with me. I'd like to say I was in love with him, but I believe I was more entranced and swept away by the lifestyle he shared with me. This generous and delightful man took me to wonderful restaurants, picked me up at the airport in a stretch limo, and always managed to entertain me with his sense of humor, bright repartee, and kind heart.

Less than a year after we were married, I realized I did not want to share my life with him. In fact, there were days I lay in bed next to him wondering how I could even spend the next twenty-four hours with him. Granted, he was bright, funny, and kind, but I did not love him and I was not physically attracted to him.

We moved together to San Diego to start a new life. Perhaps things would change. Everyone saw us as a fun-loving, compatible couple—nobody knew the truth. I could not share my feelings with another soul, and even lied to myself that things would work out since he was such a good man and he loved me.

Though I said nothing on the outside, I think he could sense that something was wrong. "One day, you'll find someone younger than me," he used to tease me. "You'll leave me for another man."

I continued to live in denial. Our life together was wonderful in so many ways. We traveled overseas together, entertained in our beautiful home, joined clubs to meet people, and made friends in our new community. I learned to feign exhaustion at the end of most days, falling asleep before he could touch me and waking up just in time to get ready for work.

After we'd been in San Diego almost a year, I started a new job and a colleague told me about a personal improvement group which sounded interesting. I went to the introductory meeting, heard words that reached out to me, and signed up immediately.

They say when the student is ready, the teacher will appear. That was definitely the case for me; I soaked up the messages and learned more about myself in a weekend than I had in the previous twenty-eight years.

Having acquired a taste for inner discovery, I signed up for the next weekend class. Several months later, I went to the intensive, seven-day program on a ranch in Northern California to face my fears and challenge myself even further.

It was during this week that I realized the inevitable and faced the fear that had been growing inside me for years: *I had to leave my husband.*

I remember standing at the edge of a cliff hundreds of feet above the ground, tethered by ropes and preparing to leap into the unknown, fear and exhilaration raging through every cell of my body. *What am I jumping into? What am I escaping?* The answers spoke loud and clear. Now I just had to find the courage to go through with it.

Seven days later, I was on a plane heading home, terrified by the prospect of what awaited me. How could I destroy the life of this man who constantly reminded me how much he adored me and how much I meant in his life?

Arriving at San Diego airport was even worse than I'd anticipated. Not only was Jeff standing in the terminal with flowers, but he'd also brought along Joey, our black lab, with balloons tied around his collar and a sign saying "Welcome Home." We hugged and made a fuss of Joey, then Jeff whisked me off in his car, telling me he'd made plans for dinner at our favorite restaurant.

An hour later I sat across from him at the restaurant, feeling sick and scared. My heart raced as he asked me about the program and what it had meant for me. I found myself telling him about the people, the exercises, the countryside, the intensity of the long days. And then the question I'd been dreading. *What had I learned about us?*

I took a deep breath and held his hand across the table, re-membering the words of a friend from the weekend. "Hold him capable," she had said. "You can't take care of his feelings. He will be fine."

"I don't think this is going to work out," I heard myself say. His face fell and his eyes teared up. "You're a wonderful man, but this isn't the relationship I want." I continued to explain my feelings as I watched his world fall apart right in front of me.

We canceled the meal, went outside and sat on a bench. Jeff cried and I tried not to take back all my words in an attempt to comfort him. Although I was tempted to take the easy way out and tell him we'd work through it, I knew I could not go back this time. I owed it to both of us to be strong and stick to my convictions.

Knowing I would end up apologizing and taking back my words if we went home, I asked him to drop me at a hotel. From the moment I got out of the car and checked into my room, it felt as though a weight had lifted from my shoulders. Although I felt sad for Jeff, at the same time I felt wonderful about myself and knew I had made the right decision in finally having the courage to walk away from a relationship that was unfulfilling and pointless.

Many times during the following days, I wanted to reach out to him and let him know I was there for him, but I forced myself to keep my distance so we could both deal with our feelings.

Two weeks later, we met at a coffee shop to discuss the separa-tion. Jeff sat down across from me, looked me in the eye and said, "It's OK. I'll be fine. Please don't worry about me anymore." And from that moment on, we established a relationship that was built on trust and mutual respect.

Fifteen years have passed now, and Jeff is a good friend. I walked away from the marriage with nothing more than what I had brought into it. I felt I had gained so many riches in our years together. He remarried a wonderful woman who is closer to his age and shares many of his interests. I went to his wedding. He sent me a gift when I remarried. We talk on the phone several times a year and I know he'll always be there for me, should I need his help.

I sometimes remember that day when I'm feeling dissatisfied with something in my life—the nauseating feeling of having to say something uncomfortable and how fearful I was of expressing myself in anticipation of the outcome. And I wonder how our lives would have worked out if I hadn't had the courage to speak up, if I'd stayed because I was afraid to make a change. I am certain we would not be living the happy, fulfilled lives we are now both living and I would never have learned the valuable lesson of *Feel the Fear and Do It Anyway®"*.

"Just tell the truth. It will save you every time."—Oprah Winfrey

Stepping into the Jungle

Ask yourself:

What do you think is the greatest benefit to you in making changes in your life?

Where in life do you resist change? Why do you think that is?

What beliefs are you holding that limit your viewpoint? Whose opinions and expectations are you carrying around as your own?

What barriers are you placing in your own way? What would happen if you removed them?

What are you grateful for?

Who are the guides in your life? What people, places, books, teachers and mentors are giving you the support you need right now?

Notes

CHAPTER 5
Have the Right Attitude

"I was ahead in the slalom. But in the second run, everyone fell on a dangerous spot. I was beaten by a woman who got up faster than I did. I learned that people fall down, winners get up and Gold Medal winners just get up faster."—Bonnie St. John

It is your attitude that determines whether you are a winner or a loser. Choose the winning side. It's always more interesting.

Are You Consistent?

I've never been known for my consistency. I once took it as a badge of merit when an employer told me the most consistent thing about me was my inconsistency. But the secret to change is that you have to be consistent. You have to consistently remind yourself that you can change, and consistently step up to taking new actions, creating new thoughts and pathways through the places where you feel small, where you doubt your capability, where you limit the expression of the life you want to live. Consistency is the key to any kind of lasting change. But I acknowledge it may not be easy.

You've heard people say "but I've always done it that way", and may even have said it yourself. But there is another way. You can change your language to reflect that 'up until now I've done it that way.' Change is as easy as making up your mind to do something differently. Breaking the bad habits of a lifetime takes time, so be gentle with you. When inconsistencies occur, gently steer yourself back onto the right path.

Keep the goal in mind.

Avoid the Potholes

Many people have created a whole opera of behaviors that keep them rooted in their desire to please other people, their fear of speaking up for what they want, need, or desire, or because they're afraid to show their weaker side. These include:

◊ Doing things because you thought you had to, you should, or you just couldn't say no.

◊ Letting others abuse your generosity because you desperately want to be liked.

◊ Complaining all the time.

◊ Daydreaming about being rescued.

◊ Neglecting your own needs.

◊ Making excuses for inexcusable behavior.

◊ Not admitting you were wrong.

◊ Manipulating others to get what you want.

◊ Hesitating to speak up.

◊ Being defensive when confronted.

◊ Being a sore loser.

◊   Wishing for something different, but doing nothing to change things.

◊   Calling yourself stupid.

◊   Denying your creativity.

◊   Eating too much.

◊   Drinking too much.

◊   Refusing to exercise.

◊   Making jokes about yourself.

◊   Apologizing for your existence.

People fear admitting these things because of being seen as inadequate, weak, stupid, or boring. Fearing they'll be rejected, abandoned, or ridiculed. In short, being vulnerable, and no one wants that. So people suffer in silence. These are the potholes of our existence.

Self-doubt is the biggest killer of BIG ideas. You second-guess, cheat on yourself, and wonder why nothing seems to be working.

Franklin D. Roosevelt once said that *the only limit to our realization of tomorrow will be our doubts of today.*

It doesn't matter where your self-doubt comes from, which stories or excuses you tell yourself and are invested in keeping. What matters is your ability to go beyond, to take actions that will lead you toward becoming more adept at handling your fears. Learning how to trust yourself is the greatest gift you can give to you.

"Find the courage to suffer happiness."—Noah Ben Shea

Keep Smiling

Many survivors will tell you that their ability to laugh at themselves was a major factor in their ability to survive. Learn how to lighten up on life. Most people take themselves too seriously, including me. Looking foolish, feeling ridiculous, is part of letting go. We are all afraid of looking like a fool, and yet it was the fool in the medieval court who held the King or Queen's secrets. He was seen as harmless so they told him everything. He was in fact, a powerful person. When you act like a fool, yes, you may not be considered serious, but here's the thing. Many serious people actually admire the ability to let go and behave with abandon.

Did you know that children laugh over two hundred times a day? Adults laugh perhaps six or seven. Some don't ever laugh. That's the saddest thing of all.

Laughter is a gift. It is the cleansing of the soul, a time to let your body feel like it's on vacation. When was the last time you had a good belly laugh? It's one of life's greatest exercise routines. They even have laughter clubs that began in India and have spread around the world. Being able to laugh at the ridiculousness of life has been one of the greatest blessings of my life.

Expressing your physical self carelessly, making silly jokes or silly observations, is liberating. It drives my daughters mad when I behave in a silly fashion. Of course, they don't call it silly, they just think it's plain old stupid and embarrassing, even if no one else is in the room. I have learned to love having fun, making fun, and laughing like crazy. I have been known to say something really stupid at the table, and to find my own jokes so hilarious that I laugh until I cry. Then I get everyone else around the table to laugh hysterically too as they watch me having a meltdown.

One morning, I woke my then eleven-year-old daughter for school. She was having a hard time with a particular school in Paris because she felt totally out of place, and I knew she did not want to get up because it was physical fitness day. She told me that the idea of physical fitness at the school was to play ping-pong, also known as table tennis, or badminton, and since coordination is not her strong suit, she was reluctant to make a fool of herself. So I crawled into bed with her and told her the story of Ping and Pong, the Chinese acrobats. I was so caught up in the ridiculousness of Ping and Pong that we both started to laugh hysterically until the tears were running down our faces.

I have created many moments like this in my children's lives. It is good for me. Laugh until you cry. It's a cleansing of the soul. Learn how to play again. I take Pilates three times a week. I call it *Gymboree for adults*. You get to play with springs and straps and rollers and balls while doing something that's good for your body. I feel great afterwards and I've never looked better.

You are on your way to living a joyful life.

Iyanla Vanzant once said "When you smile, your body feels like it's on vacation." It made everyone in the room smile. When we smile or laugh, we reduce the stress hormones and ultimately, we live longer. Laughter means spontaneous release of stress. When was the last time you had a good belly laugh until you cried? When was the last time you smiled at a stranger? When was the last time you behaved in a silly, unfettered way? When we are going through change, we need uplifting as much, if not more, than usual. Even when you feel overwhelmed, when the negativity monster has you firmly in it's grasp, try to step outside yourself for a minute and see how ridiculous it all is.

Change is the only constant we can depend on. Our emotional life rises and falls based on our thinking, our expectation and our past history. We're conditioned to misery, and we need to recondition ourselves towards happiness. We're putting money in the bank every time we smile. A deposit of good times is a thousand times better invested than a withdrawal of misery. So next time you are considering whether your misery is worth hanging onto, consider this - every time you allow your negative emotions to run your life, you are reducing your lifespan. Every time you allow your positive emotions to come out, you are rewiring your brain for longevity.

Life is for the living, and for enjoying. No one wrote down that we were meant to suffer. But for many, suffering has become the cloak they wear to justify their existence. No one wants to hang out with misery. Everyone wants to hang out with joy. So smile more often, and let your body know that every day is a holiday.

Humor is an affirmation of man's dignity, a declaration of man's superiority to all that befalls him.—Romain Gary

Age and Attitude

"I love the idea of fifty, because the best is yet to come. I am going to live to be one-hundred, because I want to, and I am going to go on learning....This has been the best year of my life."—Shirley MacLaine

84

I couldn't finish this chapter without talking about age and attitude. I'm in my fifties, and quite frankly, it surprises the hell out of me that I've reached this age. When I looked at my mother in her fifties, she struck me as growing old. Recently, I showed my daughter a picture of her grandmother at age fifty-five. When I asked how old she thought her grandmother was in that picture, she said, "Eighty." My mother was heavier in both her body and in her thinking as well. By sixty-one she was dead from a heart attack. Now that I'm in my late-fifties, the surprise is that I'm here, and more importantly, I'm healthy. That's why I took the tagline, "It's not about Age…It's about Att!tude." At this age, attitude goes a long way.

I have been called The Fearless Lady because I step up to the challenges of my life with the courage to face whatever it is I need to face. Recently, I attended a motivational training that included going out into the streets asking for money without giving any reason why people should give it to me. You can imagine the kind of fear that evoked in me, and for the two hundred plus attendees who were part of this experience. But I took the task on and at the end of the night I raised $38. It wasn't much, but it wasn't about the money, it was about my ability to face the fear of asking for what I wanted. (At that conference, a total of $20,000 was raised from strangers and it all went to Make A Wish Foundation. The power of asking for what you want is extraordinary.)

I followed Susan Jeffers advice to *Feel the Fear and Do It Anyway*™, and that's exactly what I have been doing. As I approached these strangers asking for money, I thought: be yourself. That's all you can do. In my younger years, there was no chance I would have ever undertaken this, but I have done lots of other things that would have made some people cringe at the thought. At the time, I wasn't sure if it was courageous or stupid—probably a mixture of both. But more importantly it was my attitude that carried the night.

The wisdom of years gives me a certain advantage in confronting challenges because I earned the courage to get to where I am today. I developed Att!tude. I like being in midlife. It is a tremendously fulfilling and freeing time if you are willing to take the steps through the jungle of chaos and confusion that sometimes dominate your thinking.

When I reached midlife and plunged into redefining myself *again*, I had no idea my experience would pave the way for my first motivational company *Fearless Fifties*, which was uniquely tailored to my sister travelers in midlife. When I began, I had nothing more than a good idea to take my experiences in getting past the fear, and use them to motivate and inspire others to move past their own limitations. Turning 50 was a milestone, and at 54, I was looking down a long barrel that said I needed to do something more fulfilling with my life. Although I had written books, traveled the globe, sung on stage and taken up martial arts in midlife, it wasn't enough. I wanted more. I wanted to be a teacher when I was a child, and I took my degree in history in order to do just that, but I never made that happen. Instead, I did all kinds of other things, but the idea of teaching still remained. I wanted to share the knowledge I had gained on entering my own jungle and coming out the other side. And along the way, I had to take another deep breath, say I know nothing about running a business, but I will learn. I stepped into the abyss and said it will be what it will be. Three years later, I'm still learning. I'm very proud of all I've created in my lifetime, and especially proud of this part of the journey.

Fifty is a celebration of freedom—it reminds me of a saying I heard somewhere, "When I was thirty, I worried what people thought of me. When I was forty, I didn't give a damn what people thought about me. When I was fifty, I realized no one was thinking about me in the first place." In other words, this is personal. Gone are the self-conscious, am-I-good-enough attitudes. Fifty brings a fresh perspective to life, one that a younger woman just can't fake. To reach fifty is to tuck five decades of wisdom and experience into your pocket.

In our twenties and thirties, our baby-boomer generation made great strides for women, and in our forties, we began to believe there would be more equality, more respect, and a more fulfilling life for our daughters and ourselves. We boomers have accomplished much, but there is more to do. But at this time of life, we are stepping into something new. We are creating a unique paradigm of aging. We are moving up in our advancing years with a strength and vitality that has never been seen before. We are healthy, fully engaged in the world, and anticipate years of activity and celebration. This generation has always believed we can be much more than other people think we are. We are the first generation to truly embrace, in large numbers, the concept that we really *can* have it all, and that we can change the world. Of course, the world may not have bowed down to our self-confidence, but nevertheless, we keep on keeping on (as we were fond of saying).

In this culture, there is a deep-seated belief that menopausal women have left their vital years behind, but I say pshaw! to that. The spark that lives in everyone is finally finding free expression at this age. We are now more creative, more passionate, and more deeply committed to changing the world than ever before because we are free of the constraints of procreation and lives defined by family and career. Moving through the jungle of life and entering menopause, we must acknowledge and understand the incredible power we hold in our hands. We must destroy the myth that we are old, used up, and destined to slip quietly into that dark night.

We boomers are strong, vibrant, and powerful women who are just beginning to figure out what we are really made of. As women, we have borne children, taken care of the family, supported partners and parents, and kept communities alive and vibrant. These are our gifts to the world, and in our fifties, the gift we give ourselves is to use these strengths to live our best lives NOW. We have not only earned it, we deserve it, and must honor and respect who we are in the world so we can continue to give to others in a meaningful way.

The world is consumed with violence and injustice, and as I write this book, the economy of the United States has fallen apart and it is in the worst crisis since the Great Depression. It is abundantly clear that what is needed is strong leadership with clear thinking and a focus on healing a world that is in transition. Like all change, it will take time to improve, and my hope is that you are reading this at a time when that change is evident. The world needs people who are skilled at organization, diplomacy, nurturing, decision-making, scheduling, budgeting, and crisis management. It is precisely those skills that have allowed women to endure through the ages. These are the skills you learn as you mature, and if there is any doubt in anyone's mind about who to hire to make the turnaround, ask me. Yes, we women have the answers. It is the female brain and wisdom that will make the difference. The chaos of today will be healed by the wisdom of women who are now in midlife. We are the pioneers in this process. When we bring together our collective wisdom there is no telling what miracles we can perform.

Having the right att!tude is what living a good life is all about.

"If you are NOT living on the Edge, you are taking up too much room."—Bob Proctor

Tales from the Trail
"The Wisdom of Loneliness as a Fearless Fifty"
—Claudia Scott

Every year I make a solo pilgrimage to a place I have never been. It is a ritual that began on my fiftieth birthday when I yearned to be alone to celebrate the milestone rite of passage that writer Victor Hugo defined as the invisible boundary between the end of youth and the beginning of old age.

In 2007, I chose Alberta, Canada as the destination for my weeklong sojourn of reflection and renewal. Accompanied only by a new journal, escaping daily must-do-lists and e-mails, I have a sense of freedom that is indescribable to those who have never done the same. The solitude is delicious as I go wherever impulse beckons.

One of those whims led me to a small shop in Banff. Being the only customer, I received a somber acknowledgment from the salesclerk when I entered. She was so obviously distressed that I asked what was wrong.

My concern opened an emotional floodgate. Stifling sobs, Cecile shared that only a few months prior she had left her family in Nova Scotia to live with a man whom she had not known for very long. Things were not as promised. His infidelities, lies, sudden rages, and lack of steady employment made life miserable. Yet she was too ashamed to tell her parents and faraway friends.

"Cecile, go home now," I pleaded as I gave reasons to run, not walk, to the nearest exit. I waited for the excuses I have heard countless times from women in abusive relationships.

Still, her tearful, honest whisper went right to my gut. "I'm afraid that no one else will want me. I am terrified of being lonely for the rest of my life." Much as I wanted to comfort Cecile, I could not give hollow assurances that someone else would indeed come along. Sometimes the ones worthy of us never appear.

To the contrary, my spontaneous though gentle admonition rather stunned me. "Life is lonely for everyone, Cecile, whether you have a partner or not. People let you down. Even those who truly love you can betray you in ways that cause searing pain. They leave you. They die. You cannot escape loneliness. Don't ever put the burden of keeping you from it onto someone else. It is not their job."

Phew! Where did that come from? When did I begin to believe that accepting loneliness is a key component to a happy life? Is it maturity that allows me to know that people, things, and situations in the outer world change constantly, and that is okay? Even if it hurts. When did I become wise?

Although I cherish and enjoy several loving and nurturing relationships, in the end I know it is only my personal integrity and faith that I can count on to get me through this life of challenges. I feel fortunate to have finally released my expectations that others can satisfy a core of joy that only I can fill. I also feel more inner peace because I have surrendered (admittedly after decades of trial and error).

I lovingly shared with Cecile that the first step to healing is to simply acknowledge the feelings of sadness that sometimes overwhelm people. Then you need to replace that sorrow with meaningful purpose and action.

I encouraged her not to be afraid of being lonely at times, but rather to embrace it for its gifts. Pain can be a great catalyst for needed changes. By taking time to listen to that still small voice within, you always receive honest answers about your highest good.

Could Cecile possibly understand? Could she appreciate the power that I, more than twice her age, feel by accepting that whatever happens, I can face it? Even if I kick and scream as I do?

Was Cecile too young and fragile to believe in her ability to survive on her own? Had she been scarred in other ways that prevented her from comprehending? Would she ever get to a point of trust in herself? Many don't.

Maybe I so wanted her to believe me because only recently had I once again proved to myself that what I was sharing was possible. When a beloved nephew suddenly died, I almost suffocated from the deepest grief I have ever known. But even as I was choking on anguish, I still experienced many joyous moments mingled in with the dark days that had me often inwardly, and sometimes outwardly, wailing with rage over the loss.

I received immeasurable love from others and was able to give it to those who also needed comfort. I even laughed often as I was enveloped by precious memories. I had a renewed appreciation for the time left with others whom I love. It was a chance to practice inner faith when my outer world was crumbling. These are the true gifts to my soul.

When Cecile thanked me for being the angel who appeared when she most needed one, I knew it was really I who had been given an important life lesson through our serendipitous encounter.

I was finally becoming a *Sophia*—a mature woman of wisdom who understands that one of the main challenges in life is successfully surviving the inevitable losses and loneliness everyone faces; successfully being fearless of a future with no guarantee that those we love the most will be with us as we face it.

I also have to admit that, before fifty, I had only been practicing. I didn't know that I didn't know. And although I am still learning, on that beautiful Canadian spring day, in a moment of grace, I did know. And I hoped that someday Cecile would know it also.

Getting to know yourself, examining your life, and questioning everything is easy to avoid or delay when there are corporate ladders to climb, bills to pay, and children to raise. But if you don't start now, when will you start?

Stepping Into The Jungle

Ask Yourself:

Where in your life do you doubt yourself? What are the negative voices saying to you?

Do you contradict yourself when asking for what you want? Do you mumble, run circles around it, give-in to other people's demands too easily, or are just afraid because you 'know' you won't get it?

Do you do things because you think you should do them, or because you feel obligated? Is someone else running your show?

Do you have a hard time admitting you are wrong? Do you refuse to admit your mistakes because you think it's a weakness? What would it look like if you saw it as a strength?

Are you anxious that others will find out you are just faking it? No matter how successful you are, do you feel that you'll get caught out. What would it look like to own your success?

PART 2
CHOOSE THE RIGHT PATH

Notes

CHAPTER 6
Examine Your Excuses

▲▲

"The trouble with words is that you never know whose mouths they've been in."—Dennis Potter

We are all the product of our environment and the conditions under which we've been raised. We are also the product of other people's opinions and expectations. Stop listening to their voices.

What Stories Do You Tell Yourself?

We are all a collection of stories. Some of them are short stories and some of them are epic novels. Whatever length these stories are, that's our history and our influences. These are the conglomeration of experiences that make us who we are. Many times these stories were handed down to us by the people who were the most formative influences on our life; parents, grandparents, teachers, siblings, friends and employers. We learned who we are by what they said about us. We learned what we could do by using them as examples. We learned what the world was all about by seeing it through their eyes. And many times, we didn't stop to question if it was right or wrong!

When I was growing up my father told me a hundred thousand times (I didn't keep count, but it was a lot!) that I wouldn't amount to much. I would end up a waste of time, with an unhappy marriage, just like his, and I'd be broke, just like him. I'd get pregnant and not know who the father was, just like my mother, and I'd always be disappointed by life, because that's just the way it is. Interspersed with this 'wisdom' came raging alcoholic abuse because I dared to step out of line, because I dared to question, and because I didn't know any better. My mother didn't help matters. Her best advice was to stay out of his way. Don't rock the boat. And definitely, don't bother to dream, because you will be disappointed. In elementary school, my math teacher told me I was a complete idiot because I could never understand the simplest math problems, and my English teacher told me I was lazy because I never handed my homework in on time. We were poor so I learned that the only way to get things was to steal them, because my mother stole whisky from the distillery and my father stole food and whisky from the docks he worked in. I learned how to lie to get what I wanted because nobody ever told you the truth about what was going on, and years later, when I discovered their stories, I understood why. They were too ashamed to step forward and reveal who they truly were.

If you grew up with a large dose of negativity, then that is your reality. If you grew up listening to people complain all the time, berate other people, diminish your expectations and pigeon-hole you according to their limited beliefs, then you suffer the consequences of that. You grow smaller. You don't believe in yourself. You limit your world because of these influences. Or you rebel.

I chose to rebel, but it took its toll. I did come home pregnant, just like my mother. I did get caught stealing, just like my father. I buried myself in drugs and alcohol to dull the pain, just like my father and my mother, and I didn't believe I would ever amount to much. How wrong can you be? These stories led me down a path that was not of my choosing, or so I thought.

Iyanla Vanzant, a wonderful, spirited teacher, said, "You can't be in both passion and pissocity." I love that word. Pissocity. We are all pissed off at some level. Until you express your pissocity in a clear, focused way, you cannot express your passion. I'm an expert in that. My therapist of many years told me it was my rage that was driving me forward but it would only carry me so far. She was correct. My anger has been a major driving force and a very destructive energy—these extremes crippled me for many years.

But here's an interesting thing about anger. It's fear driven. When I'm angry, it's usually in reaction to something that pushes my buttons. I'm out of control because I'm trying desperately to make sense of something I don't understand. It's the "I don't know what to do" alarm, and the unknown is a scary place to be.

Anger wears many masks. It gets hidden under the search for approval, self-neglect, helplessness, and depression, under the need for perfectionism and the absolute terror of maybe making a mistake. It also hides behind passive-aggressive behavior which sabotages even our best efforts, and emotional disconnection, so that nothing can hurt.

People are afraid of anger. They haven't been taught how to express it, and most of the time it comes out in negative and destructive forms. Anger is fear expressing itself in a very loud way, but instead we have been taught to stuff it, swallow it, bury it... but it keeps coming up anyway.

Anger will always look for a way out. It is a transforming agent. As long as you contain your anger, you will not be able to experience joy and passion either above or below the waist. Sexual dysfunction and lack of interest is often due to unexpressed anger. If anger cannot find a way to be released, it consumes you. My anger was the splintered, broken shards of me that begged to be healed. It was my rage at the unfairness of life. The great cloud of despair that threatened to swallow me whole was my own inner yearning to be set free.

Learn how to express your anger. Write it out, speak it out, beat up a pillow, open your mouth and roar—but not *at* anyone. That's not productive, and will possibly lead to more frustration and remorse. Anger needs an expression or it will kill. Literally. Recent studies have shown that cancer is one of the side effects of anger. This is your anger, it is important that you own it without spewing it around. If you do, you abuse the person whose receiving it, multiplying the negativity and remorse you will have to face later. I've been guilty of that too many times in my life.

Watch what you do, and how you do it. I gradually began listening to what I said, watching what I did, taking a deep breath when someone said I was wrong before defending myself. Eventually I was even able to recognize my own responsibility when appropriate. I had to give up being right all the time and making other people wrong. I had to get past the place of choking on my own anger, guilt, shame, worthlessness, and judgments about other people. Most of the time, it wasn't about them, but it was about me. My own self-loathing was firmly in the way. I had to find a way to move beyond the terrible fears and insecurities that kept me in that broken place.

Growing up, I was a victim—of other people's unhappiness, frustration, and depression, I used that experience to create my own pattern of misery. This is not uncommon. The secrets and lies of generations get handed down like heirlooms. There were many reasons to believe that I was a worthless human being. It was conveyed to me on a daily basis, through actions, words, and attitudes. I clung to that notion for a very long time. There were hundreds of excuses to keep me safe, but even I grew tired of hearing them. I wanted something different, but didn't know what that looked like. I only knew I had to have the courage to stand up for myself, and I could no longer neglect my own needs. In the beginning it was messy. I had no role models to follow and the road map was anything but clear. And I was able to see clearly that some of my choices were destructive and left deep scars on the lives of others.

In early adulthood, I couldn't give myself a break if I tried. I truly believed I didn't deserve it. I was worthless and absolutely sure of it.

But I was completely wrong.
I had trained myself into believing those things. I needed to retrain myself out of these false beliefs.

There is a passage from the Bible: "The sins of the fathers shall be visited upon the children." I'm sure there are many interpretations of that, but for me it meant I was forced to heal several generations of pain that had been dumped on me by my family. It was at this time I realized that all those years of trying to be good enough for others, was really about trying to prove to myself I was worthy of love and acceptance.

This anger to prove that I could do it, was the anger that would eventually save me. It was an incredible fire and power that burned inside of me and wouldn't take no for an answer. I had to prove to myself, and to my father who had said I would never amount to much, that he was wrong. I've spent my lifetime with that same impulse in my marriage and in everything I do. I am learning how to allow that I am good enough without proving anything more in life. After five children, five books, a black belt in martial arts and a short career as a singer, I don't feel a need to prove anything, except to say I can do it. I felt the fear and did it anyways. I would not accept NO for an answer, and I would not allow my fears to stop me. Anger transformed my life because it pushed me always onwards. It was my saving grace, and my worst enemy.

We are all trained into fear, so we can all be trained out of it.

When do you catch yourself telling the same old stories about why you can't do something? There's a familiarity to the story. Not enough money, not enough relationship, my health isn't good, I'm too old, too fat, too tired. I used to dream about a future that was better, but that was then, and this is reality. I can't have it. I'm not capable, I'm not worthy, I'm not good enough, I'm not qualified, I'm not creative, I'm not, I'm not, I'm not. Is that the Yadda Yadda of your life?

If so, you're not alone. 99.9% of people have that conversation almost daily.

You know that life is all about choices and we have the freedom to make good ones or bad ones. So why then do so many make bad choices? Usually it's fear or insecurity that's leading the charge.

I've been married for 27 years and counting, but it hasn't always been easy. Several years ago I was ready to divorce my husband. I blamed him for all kinds of things, and I blamed him for creating the life we were living. It was all his fault.

Most of my life I was pretty good at blaming other people, blaming circumstances and blaming the past for the present predicament. In my marriage, we were constantly fighting about money, about where to live, and how to live. I wanted one thing, he wanted another. And then one day, in the midst of a huge fight, he said something quite profound that I had not heard before.

He said, "You made the choice to be with me!"

For some reason, that phrase slammed home. For the first time in my thirty-eight year life I truly understood that we all make choices about where we want to be in life. I had made my choice to be with him and whatever unhappiness I was experiencing, it was my choice.

You will have different stories, but they all have a familiar ring to them. We watch television and movies where we witness the anger and sadness of the human experience. We suffer the indignities of human existence in a tangential way, but the main reason for viewing them is they make us feel better because our lives are not as bad as that! But we also watch the movies that bring us joy and give us hope for a better tomorrow because that's the stories we are hoping to recreate in our own lives. We are constantly on the lookout for something better in our material life upgrading our physical existence to something more; a bigger car, bigger house, more gadgets, clothes, toys. The list is endless. Our wants always outstrip our needs, and we believe them to be important because we're told they are by the society in which we live.

Choices are what dominate whether we have a good life, a bad life or an okay life. We make decisions that seem right for the moment, and frequently, there is an element of regret around the choices. We wish we had thought about it more, had taken more time to consider all the aspects, and had known what we know now.

We have all made choices that were wrong. It is a fundamental fact of life that we will make mistaken choices. Sometimes we run into things blindly and hope that we will end up okay, but frequently find ourselves in trouble. In my own life, I made some very foolish choices that got me pregnant and unable to figure out who the father was because I had been having too much fun with several guys at the same time. Or flying from London to Philadelphia, then taking a Greyhound bus from Philadelphia to San Diego because I was in love with someone who was clearly not in love with me. After a three-day drunk, we ended up on a highway in Ensenada, Mexico with a wrecked car and no money to return to England.

We build stories in our minds to lend credibility to our position. When you believe you're no good, then you'll literally create the life around that. All of these women above inherently believed they were flawed. A teacher in school tells you you're useless so many times you believe it, and years later, when you've forgotten the teacher, there's a little part of your unconscious that says you will never amount to much. So you go out of your way to create situations that allow you to continue living that story.

We are all full of stories. Stories from our past, stories we tell ourselves, stories that other people tell us, and the stories are the things that pull us down because we believe them.

I'll bet you can give me an example of negative stories you heard about yourself in the past that you believe to be true.

Whose Opinions/Expectations Are You Living By?

When we examine our lives we must ask ourselves "Whose doing the talking?" We are conditioned by our past and we are conditioned by the fears, self-doubts and anxieties that belong to other people.

I was raised by two people who lived every day of their life in fear; every decision they ever took was based in fear. As a manual worker in the docks, my father lived during a time when you could not depend on work being there. If you've ever seen the movie On The Waterfront with Marlon Brando,that was the kind of situation my father lived with. Men standing around on the dock waiting to be picked out of a line, being paid by the day instead of a salary. Spending his last penny on a drink so he could forget how bad it was. My mother had two children before she married my father and she wasn't very excited about having more, but they took no precaution and she ended up getting pregnant three times with him. On the third one, she was told he would kill himself if they had more children, so she tried to get rid of it until she was five months pregnant. My brother was born severely retarded. She lived with the shame and the guilt for the rest of her life. She was afraid for me because she didn't want me to end up the same way. But she couldn't relay that message to me and instead I lived with her fear unexpressed through controlling behavior, and a refusal to speak about things.

We are all of influenced by the people around us for good and bad. One of the best influences in my life was a single mother raising four children, who always took time for my brothers and I during our most chaotic years, and who spent her spare time helping children with disabilities. An English teacher who tried to stop me leaving school at fifteen because she saw something greater in me than I saw in myself; a social worker who knew I was much smarter than I believed. A husband who saw me long before I saw myself.

So how do you change the stories? You start by changing the stories you tell yourself. The stories you believe are true and are not. Then begin creating your own story. The one you are building for yourself.

What are Your Avoidance Techniques?

Knowing that we are living out stories we've inherited is one thing. Doing something different is another. We say we are comfortable knowing what we know, doing what we do, and living how we live. But are you? Are you satisfied with how life is right now? If so, I'm not sure you would be reading this book. My guess is you're looking for answers but you don't know yet what the question is.

Change is uncomfortable. We avoid it like the plague, usually waiting until something comes in from outside influences to make us take another look at what is working or not in our lives. It could be divorce, losing a job, ill-health, a crisis with our children, our parents, or a spouse. There are as many ways in which the universe gets our attention as there are stars in the sky, and I'm sure right now you can think of a few good reasons why you can't deal with change right now. The timing is bad, there's not enough money, I just need to wait for something else to happen. Excuses are rampant in our lives, and we embrace them as if they were the gospel of our life.

Remember in the early part of the book I gave you the opera of behaviors. If we're using the opera metaphor, it's the aria you sing whenever you are confronted with your fears. You can find a thousand things to keep you busy, keep you distracted, and keep you from implementing steps that would lead you to a more positive outlook on life. The (dis)comfort zone is seductive. We think that it has always been that way, and it will always be that way. Being a Master of Procrastination, these excuses keep you from truly living the life you want. Much better the devil you know than the devil you don't know. But my response to that is "why would you want to live in hell?"

Stories are language pictures. When we change the language we change the picture. Can you 'see' how that would affect your life? Change the language and you change the picture. We'll talk more about that later in the book. The way you think about your stories is critical to becoming Fearless. We all make choices based on how we perceive ourselves. Let the stories you tell yourself come from your authentic source, not from someone else's idea of who, what and why you are what you are.

Tales from the Trail
"Drowning in Anger" – Jacqueline Wales

I heard you crying as if from the bottom of a very deep well, and as I struggled to shake off my sleepy head, I glanced at the clock. It said two a.m.

"Right on time," I murmured.

Staggering across the cold floor to the kitchen, I warmed up the bottle from the refrigerator. When I returned you were in full soprano belt. It was cold in the room, so I wrapped you in a shawl and pulled the bedcovers up over my legs. After you had taken half a bottle, you pushed it away and began to cry again. I thought it must be your diaper, so I changed you and still you cried. "Not again," I said pleadingly. "I'm tired. Just go back to sleep." But you had no intention of going back to sleep.

The room shrank to the size of a postage stamp as you continued crying. I picked you up and began pacing. The bricks on the wall outside looked awfully close. "Shush!" I admonished. "Shush. Please stop. You'll wake up the entire house." I held you tighter against me, bouncing you up and down violently. "What do you want?" I pleaded, but this only caused you to become even more anxious. I picked up the half-empty bottle but you spat it out. I put you on my shoulder and patted your back to get the wind out of you. I held you tighter and forced the bottle back into your mouth and then you vomited. You howled even more intensely. I gritted my teeth, drowning in the maelstrom of my violent temper and your insistent cries. I had to do something, so I slammed you onto the bed, leaving you shrieking and red faced. Turning away towards the window, I clawed at my face as if I were trying to rub myself out of the picture. Leaning down towards you, I hissed in your small, helpless face, "What do you want from me? What do I have to do?" Sobbing, I turned to the window and the wall and asked, What am I doing? How could I have been so stupid as to believe I could do this? Self-pity swarmed like an itch over my whole body, covering me in a depression I could not break out of. I wasn't prepared for the violence that finally took over.

The nappy pin was stuck in the cotton cloth and wouldn't go through to the other side. Your legs were working up and down like peddling a bike as I pushed and pushed, trying to get the pin through. Your cries sucked in every bit of air there was in the room, and my mouth was getting tighter and tighter as I insisted that I would get this to work. "Shut up!" I screamed with a hoarse, whispered voice, pushing the pin through to the other side and stabbing my finger.

Suddenly, without warning, I was ready to murder you. Not just the thought but the actual act of it. I picked you up and slammed you down on the bed, causing your head to bounce off the mattress. I pushed my face inches from yours, and like the girl in the film *The Exorcist*, I screamed in a contained deep, guttural voice, "Why? Why are you crying? Don't do it! Don't do it! You hear me." and I slammed my fists inches away from your head. I picked you up and began shaking you so that your head wobbled back and forth. "I don't want to feed you. I don't want to change you. I've done it and I'm not doing it anymore. You hear me? Do you hear me, you!" I was spitting on your hysterical face "I can't do this. I can't be your mother. I don't know how." Sobbing and clutching at your clothes I threw you back down on the bed again. "I hate you. I hate this mess we're in. I hate it all." You were screaming in fear and my hysteria promised to annihilate both of us. Kneeling on the floor by the side of the bed, I punched my fists into the mattress and put my face into the covers. "Get it! Get it! Get it!"

Just as suddenly as it started, the madness subsided and I scooped you up, the nappy hanging from your leg as I held you tightly to my chest. "I'm sorry," I sobbed. "I'm really sorry. I just can't do this anymore. I just can't. I'm sorry," as my tears mingled with yours and the warm rush of urine soaked the front of my nightgown. Sobbing, I held you close, putting your mouth to my empty breasts until you fell asleep in my arms.

Excerpt from *When The Crow Sings* by Jacqueline Wales, based on the author's experience of giving her child up for adoption.

Stepping into the Jungle

Ask Yourself:

What stories are you telling that are not the truth? Where do you think they started?

On a scale of 1–10, where is your 'pissocity' level? Anger is a powerful tool. How are you using yours?

What would it take for you to channel the anger into something productive? What would that be?

What are the positive effects of the energy you call anger?

What are some negative beliefs you adopted from your parents? Where did your parents live in fear, and how was it transferred to you?

Which of these negative habits has served you well? What limiting habits have actually worked to your advantage?

What decisions do you avoid and why?

What do you need to do to make the right choices for you?

CHAPTER 7
Trust Your Decisions

"The feelings of failure occur in all our lives, and the issue is who we become as a result."—Harold Kushner

Failure is only an option if you choose to see it as an end. Learn to use the word 'NEXT' and see what happens.

Stop Second-Guessing Yourself

How many times a day do you ask yourself if this is the right decision, or ask someone else what they think before you take a decision? Or perhaps you make a decision only to stop yourself from taking action because you're not sure if it's the right move? This second-guessing creates ennui. We lapse into apathy because we can't decide what we want, what we need, or what path to take. Most of the time it is caught up in our fear of failure.

Life is imperfect. We will never get it 100% right, no matter how hard you work, how much you study, or how much you are willing to sacrifice. There will always be inconsistencies. We call them mistakes and we live our lives in limitation because we are afraid of them. But the gift of mistakes are the lessons of life. And make no mistake.... gifts are abundant in our lives. We just have to learn how to accept them.

For years I didn't know how to say I was wrong because if I did, I had to admit I was weak or vulnerable and that was unacceptable. When I made a mistake, instead of seeing it for what it was; simply the wrong direction taken, I saw it as weakness. But the opposite of this is true. Admitting I could be wrong, had indeed taken the wrong direction, was a position of strength.

Life is not lived in a straight line. We zig-zag our way through life and rarely get where we want to go first time around. All skill learning is accomplished by trial and error. When you choose to avoid mistakes, you are also choosing not to live your life successfully. This is the paradox of creating the life you want. Living life successfully means we are embracing the failure. I like to say we are failing our way to success.

Thomas Edison discovered how to make a light bulb. On his journey to this discovery he made thousands of mistakes. He never saw them as faults, simply as experiments that did not give him the results he was looking for. Think of this next time you want to 'blame' yourself for making mistakes. When you go through life being excessively careful because you're afraid of doing something wrong, or making a mistake, you are aligning yourself with failure.

When you become too conscientious about what other people think, or you are constantly trying to please people, you become too sensitive to any real or imagined slights. You invite negative feedback; you invite failure, and you get exactly what you didn't want.

Mistakes are life's way of teaching us lessons. There are no right or wrong decisions, just decisions made on choices we make, and sometimes it's the wrong one. I have only one word for you to remember. "NEXT!" When you choose the wrong path, or you choose the wrong action there is only one choice. "NEXT!" signals to the brain that you made a left turn instead of a right. You are making a course correction.

Instead of telling yourself how stupid you were, how careless you are, how bad you've been, try changing the thought patterns to "Wow! That was an interesting lesson." Or "Hmm, next time I'll do it differently." If you keep running the mistake over and over in your head, then you'll constantly replay the past, which serves you no purpose other than to keep you chained to behavior that doesn't fit your needs.

Making mistakes is essential if we are to make progress in life. Of course, there are times when making a mistake is the difference between life and death. We wouldn't want the doctor to make the wrong diagnosis or the airline pilot to land badly. But viewed in the right light, your mistakes are your guides to what's not working and what you need to do to progress on your journey towards being your best self now. Remember, we fail our way to success. Without them, we learn nothing. If you think about it, we don't know everything there is to know about whatever it is you are involved with. So it's natural that we would deviate from the path from time to time.

So get some perspective on your mistakes. Did you really do something that threatened another life? Has it turned your life upside down and there is no recovery from it? Was it an embarrassment and nothing more? Learn how to forgive yourself and move on. When you have that act of forgiveness for yourself, it's amazing how quickly others will forgive you more quickly too.

Admit your mistakes. We all make them and then we move along. If someone is angry with you, then face it and make amends. Admit you were foolish. We all do stupid things and regret the foot in mouth syndrome that sometimes happen. I've done that more times than I can tell. Nobody dies from it. Let people know how sorry you are and that you've learned something valuable. People admire that in others. They will trust you again.

People ask me, "How did you learn to take fear out of your life?" The answer is, "I didn't." I learned how to deal with fear by making it my friend—by accepting it, understanding it, listening to it, and taking appropriate action based on previous experiences and reliable intuition. I learned how to embrace my fear as a lover, because ultimately going beyond it creates enormous self-love. I had been riddled with self-doubt, blame, and avoiding responsibility for my actions. I had to learn to trust that no matter how hard it was to change the experiences I was having, it would be a whole lot better on the other side. But you don't have to take my word for it. You have to try it on for size.

The reason for fearing things is all about control. You fear that you have no control over an outcome. You fear that you don't have the ability to do or say the right thing. You fear being rejected, abandoned, embarrassed, or foolish. You don't trust. The underlying message of fear is, "I don't know if I'm capable of handling this. It might be too much." It may not be a conscious thought. In fact, most of the time it's not conscious, but it lingers in the wings waiting for the opportunity to present itself. The thoughts are that you will fail, and if you succeed, it won't last. Someone will find out you were only faking it. You will be discovered as a fraud and exposed. Some very successful people struggle with the feeling that one day they will be caught and everyone will find out they are faking it.

Control is encouraged in our society. In class, you need to keep your impulses under control—raise your hand, stand in line. As you develop skills, the more control you display, the better. Whenever you were reckless, or made a mistake, you were taught to be more careful, to have some control. If you didn't, you'd get in trouble.

As a child, I was always in trouble. I talked back to my parents— trouble. I stayed out too late—more trouble. I climbed on roofs and stole things from shops—trouble. I lied about where I was, or money disappeared—trouble. And I paid for it. My father let me know that I would suffer for my troubles by beating me. I grew to be afraid of him, and to be afraid of what I could do, of my potential for destruction. But it wasn't enough to stop me. That is significant---fear of the trouble I knew was coming was *not enough* to make me change my behavior. This can often be seen in *troubled* children, and I presume that is where they get the title of troubled children. They are seekers of trouble, magnets for trouble, and creators of trouble. In my case, trouble was the only way I could cry out.

A Course in Miracles teaches that every act is either love, or a call for love. It's easy to see how that works. Help someone to cross the street---that's an act of love. One driver screams at another on the road—that's a cry for love; it's a sign that the driver is not experiencing love, because she or he is lashing out at others.

That is the behavior of someone who is empty and aching inside, who needs a hug. Now I don't recommend you pull over and try to administer one, but wouldn't it be lovely if you could? If every person who is walking around filled with fear and anger could just be scooped up and snuggled until they felt better? That is, if they allowed it to happen. My youngest daughter refused all attempts toward love whenever she was in one of her tantrums, preferring instead to hold onto the confusion and chaos. You allow in what you are comfortable with, and what you are willing to trust.

As a child who needed love, whose entire family needed to be washed in forgiveness and redemption, the only way my soul knew to shout out for love was to act completely UNlovable much of the time. That is such an amazing paradox, but it is absolutely true. When a child is stealing from you, sneaking out, staying out all night, showing up drunk or high or just pissed off, it may be hard to hear the call for love. But that was what it was. The broken young woman that I was had no language for what was happening, for what was rising up inside me that even beatings could not stop. I continued to do the wrong things until one day I awoke and asked myself, *"What* are you doing?" By then, I was six months pregnant with a child I didn't want, whose father was a forgotten ten minutes in my memory.

Today, everyone is confronted with much to be fearful about. With the collapse of the Twin Towers in New York in 2001, the world entered a new era of global warfare with undeclared enemies and random attacks that left everyone feeling vulnerable in places thought to be safe. Now, people live in a culture of fear and it is widespread, thanks to global communications. In his book *The Science of Fear*, Daniel Gardner said "irrational fear is running amok, and often with tragic results. In the months after 9.11, when people decided to drive instead of fly – believing that they were avoiding risk – road deaths rose by 1,595. Those lives were lost to fear" Everyone traffics in fear. Madison Avenue, the media, television programs, all trade on fear.

There is a constant struggle with a personal sense of identity, and people search for meaning in their lives. Much of what is sought is a result of the desire to escape the dull ache that resides in the body. The uncertainty and temporary nature of life has always been there, but now it feels even more pervasive. Many are afraid of what they are, and afraid of what they will find—out there.

Many believe if they could just find God, maybe they could find the answers to what makes life such a challenge. But the truth is, God resides exactly where you are now, and there is nothing to find. There is only YOU to find—you with your con- nection to the Divine Presence that exists in everything and everyone.

The lesson I learned early in life was that you can't trust anyone because they will disappoint and abuse you. This feeling of loss sent me careening into drugs and alcohol and looking for love in all the wrong places. I had my first drink at thirteen, at fifteen I began having sex. At sixteen, I was on probation for drug use, and my first child was born when I was nineteen, with no clue who the father was. I was heading down a slippery slope to nowhere, and nobody was there to catch me. There was no one out there I could or wanted to trust.

I have lived with paralyzing fear. I have lived with big fears, little fears, nagging fears, devastating fear, and shameful fear, and I have confronted Fear with a capital F. To the outsider looking in, my life has looked alternately dismal, glamorous, shredded, and perfect.

I made mistakes big and small, and blamed other people for all the unhappiness that was the sum of my life. I was born in poverty, but ended up in a pretty comfortable place, all the time thinking I didn't deserve it. I've had the stuff that other people crave, but it didn't make any difference. Internally, I was a quivering wreck constantly struggling to survive. I eventually realized that it wasn't the stuff out there, or the people who were making my life miserable, but the stored-up anger and resentment that was running my life.

I had to learn how to forgive, and to trust myself. To give up the control and realize the fundamental belief that I am in partnership with God, Spirit or whatever else you want to call the Divine presence. If I let go, and I trust myself, then my life is filled with more love and less fear. I am blessed in so many important ways, with a myriad of gifts that continue to illuminate my life including the ability to share what I have learned with others.

Learn how to align yourself with success. Learn how to trust that you have all the answers. You are infinitely more accomplished, more capable and more successful than you would admit to yourself. Making mistakes means your human. You are learning, growing and expanding in ever-widening circles.

Do You Think YOU'RE All Right?

Many of us spend a great deal of time asking others if it's all right. We think we are valuing their opinions, but what we are looking for is validation for our own. This is at the heart of trust your decisions.

I have a daughter who is smart, sophisticated, funny and generous but she hates making decisions when she's around me. "What do you think?" comes up a lot in our conversations and I'm always throwing it back to her. She will badger me until she gets a response she's looking for, which is usually validating what she originally set out to do. She doesn't trust that she's giving herself the best advice.

We spend our lives being influenced by other people's thinking and also being limited by other people's thinking. How many times in your life have you heard "I wouldn't do that if I were you," and then sidestepped your original decision only to find out that you should have listened to yourself. I would bet the answer is "frequently".

Many times before you ask someone's opinion, you've already made up your mind before you ask that his or her answer is not important. You're just trying to be polite. Make them feel good. This kind of opinion seeking is a waste of everyone's time and in turn, disappoints the other person when you didn't take it. So question why you are asking for someone's opinion. If it's has merit, then great. Go ahead, but if it's simply to give yourself validation, then think again.

I'm not saying it's wrong to ask for other people's opinions. In fact, in certain situations, it's critical we ask others opinion to make sure we're on the right track. Recently, I redesigned my website and changed my brand from The Fearless Fifties to The Fearless Factor, which was more expansive. We had several versions of the pages before we hit the winning formula, and I asked my subscribers what they thought worked. I got some really good feedback that helped me develop it so that everyone was on the winning side.

You Have All the Answers

Hidden in your mixed up thinking are the answers you are looking for. It is the inner knowing that all of us have when we trust ourselves. But where we get off track is when we depend on others opinions and don't listen to our inner voice of reason; the place of knowing that lives within all of us. I like to tell people who come to me for advice that I'm not going to tell you anything you don't already know. You've heard a great deal of what I'm offering a million times, but perhaps this is the first time it's actually reaching your conscious mind and you 'hear' it. The hearing is your inner knowledge. We all know what's good for us. But frequently we are living with other people's ideas of what's good for us.

So next time you ask an opinion, ask yourself why you need it? Is it a need to feel acknowledged, that there is a reason for your existence, that you are important, and that being in this world matters? If you don't feel validated, what about that matters to you. Do you feel invisible, or unimportant? What would it take for you to believe you are?

Are you seeking guidance to make it through the jungle of life?

Imagine embarking on a rainforest journey without a map, bug repellant, or a canteen of water. Anyone can agree it would be a foolhardy plan to enter an unknown jungle alone, with no supplies. Then why are you hesitant to ask for a guide through the jungle of life? Why do you put the pressure on yourself that you need to make it alone, that you should know exactly what you need and how to get it?

Everyone needs guides in life—someone who has paved the way and can teach us how to overcome circumstances and reach for success. I've had my fair share of them.

In my childhood, when everything around me was chaotic, we had a neighbor who took care of my brothers and me when my parents were either drowning in alcohol, or too busy working to pay the bills. She was my first major guide toward the possibility of a brighter future. The simple, nurturing acts of sharing a meal with us, being happy to see us no matter what time of day or night, and allowing us to participate in healthy family moments, enabled me to savor those memories and envision a future free of addiction and poverty. But I would have to travel a different road before I got there.

As I grew older, my second guide was a social worker and psychiatrist who believed I could be more than I was at that moment; who encouraged me to do things differently. As a textbook example of a troubled teen, it would have been easy to dismiss my self-destructive lifestyle as insurmountable, but she reached into my darkness and offered a lifeline of possibility and hope. She helped me open up a dream.

In my thirties, I started therapy to move beyond the stifling fear, the basement-level self-worth, and the general anxiety that life was meant to crush me. Looking back on that period, it amazes me that somehow I was that person who was so utterly baffled by life's challenges. A shiver travels down my spine as I recall that terrifying place. Working with my therapist, I began to see that I was so much more than the limited person I thought I was; that my mind had been shut to the possibilities because I was afraid of getting hurt again.

I've spent a lot of time and energy in Alcoholics Anonymous, Al-Anon, workshops, self-discovery tours, coaching, past-life regression, Gestalt, Reiki, Treiger, inner-child work, writing therapy, singing therapy, martial arts, and a whole host of other therapies that have been my guides throughout the years. I was a mess, and as I learned to stop thrashing and went beyond the survival mode that was my way of thinking, I learned how to thrive.

With all this work, I learned how to embrace fear as an incredible motivator. Every time fear shows up, you have a choice. Deal with it, or deny it. Denying it is a real kick, because that means it will have time to grow and intensify. The next time you encounter it, be assured it will be harder to ignore. Fear will not be denied; it will control you until you challenge it.

With my background of abuse, I felt invisible a lot of the time. I felt that no one was seeing the real me. So I spent a greater part of my life asking for approval. It has been the rope around my neck, frankly. Always seeking someone else to validate what and who you are is a set-up for failure. You will be disappointed if you don't get it. You will feel unsupported if you don't get the results you were looking for.

The problem with this way of thinking is that it is self-perpetuating. When we look outside ourselves for the validation, we don't always get what we want. The hardest place to look for answers is outside your self. By placing the burden on someone else to fill a need that can only be filled by you, you are setting yourself up for disappointment. The next step is to KNOW that you already have all you need inside of you right now, as you'll discover as you go through this book.

My husband likes to say the only time I ask his opinion when I'm getting dressed to go out is because I know in my heart, whatever it is I'm wearing isn't working. I already know the answer. He's right. I've already decided that something isn't working, and I probably don't look good, but I just need validation. That's why we ask opinions – it's because we want our feelings, our thoughts, our actions validated.

But you have to be careful with this. There are too many people who are happy to give their opinion and you will be bouncing from pillar to post as you try to follow them. Remember, not all opinons are equal. You have to look behind the scenes to understand where it is coming from. If someone says 'don't do it,' consider the source. Don't be led by other people's expectations. Let your gut tell you what's needed. If someone gives you advice, listen to your inner self. If the advice contributes to your well-being and the successful accomplishment of what you desire, then by all means, follow what they say. But like they used to say back in the hippie days, "question authority." Don't' follow blindly, but learn how to trust your own decisions.

Trust your inner wisdom and you will learn how to trust your decisions.

"Don't believe what your eyes are telling you. All they show is limitation. Look with your understanding, find out what you already know, and you'll see the way to fly."—Richard Bach

Tales from the Trail
"Today Is the Day"—Ann Gordon

I have been thinking about writing this Fearless essay for months and keep thinking: "What do I have to say about being fearless?" I can tell you so many stories of what I have done to overcome my fears in life. Going through a divorce, being remarried, having my husband lose his job the day our first child was born prematurely and was in the Intensive Care Unit for ten days. I can tell you how I went hiking and made it through the *lemon squeeze*, or about the time I took my three young children (ages six, three, and two) to New York City by myself so they could say they have a fun mom. Then there are all of the things that I do on a daily basis, plus more. I am up at 5am to exercise, I get three kids ready for daycare and school, I work full time.....blah blah blah blah is all I have to say to that.

So, I am out on my walk this morning, pitch black at 5:15am, and the sun rises at 6:15am, mace in hand, and lights on my head, and really thinking about this and what fearless means to me, and I just kept running up against the wall of *hero cover-up*. That's right, the hero cover-up. I do all these great things so everyone thinks I am a superwoman, I am the hero. I challenge myself to prove to you that I am strong, the look-at-me, I-can-do-it syndrome, and, really, when all is said and done, none of that matters. Without question, the most fearless thing I can do in my life is ask for help, something I am afraid to do.

I have never asked for help; I am too busy doing it by myself, whatever *it* is. If you ask anyone, I am an amazing woman—I do it all. On the outside, it may appear that way, but honestly, I don't ever feel amazing, no matter what I have done or am about to do. I kind of feel small in the world, unnoticed and unsure of who I really am.

You know, living fearlessly is really living toward your hopes, dreams, and goals in life—none of which I have ever done. I have always been too busy taking care of someone else's dreams and focusing on what their needs are. I have also been too busy putting on my hero suit so you can't see who or what I am, and especially not how scared and lonely I am. My biggest fear is that I will take care of you and you will take advantage of my giving and then throw me away like a piece of trash. This *has* happened. I give and give until I am used up, broken down, and empty, wondering how I ever got here and if I will ever get out.

So after many tears and heartaches, I find the strength to once again trudge the road to a happy destiny—I tell myself that to keep going. It is hard work to get out of that feeling, struggle to live life, put on my hero outfit so the world sees me as okay, and then realize that I have hopes and dreams, all of which I want to come true.

Eventually it happens, though—I find someone who needs me and I throw away all that I want to be, I disregard myself to the point that the cycle completes itself again. I have battled this pattern and depression my whole life. I have had suicidal thoughts since I was nine-years-old, somehow managing to bounce back, only to loop back into that destruction of giving myself away.

Sadly, I see that I devoted my life to living for others. My life has been for you, whomever my latest needy person may be. I don't share my dreams because I don't think they are as important as yours. I don't pursue my goals because I am focused on fulfilling yours. This has been a very sad way to live the first half of my life; I refuse to duplicate it in the second half. So what do I do from here? Where do I go?

This is where *fearless* becomes true for me. Today I am committed to living my dreams. I have to throw myself into hope, stop putting myself aside for you, and live my life for ME, no matter how uncomfortable that may be.

The words are simple, but actually practicing this way of life is not. I have three young children and a full-time job. I have chosen a dream future—coaching others to make changes in their life to reflect what they want in their life. Now that I am learning how to follow my heart, I want to share that journey with others.

So where do I go from here? What step do I take? I have found that the answers come if I imagine what advice I would give to a client—what would I do if you came to me and asked for help? I would tell you that you can do whatever you dream of doing, that you are worthy of achieving your goals. I would tell you that you are deserving, smart, and capable of doing whatever it is you want to do. Then, I would have to tell you, and myself, the only thing that is stopping you is *you*—so get the hell out of the way.

Today is the day for me to make a change, to recognize that I have dreams and they can come true. Today is the day I live fearlessly and ask for help on my life's journey.

Today is the day.

Today is the day to begin. A year from now, where do I dream of being? On my own, with my three kids, living a life of emotional and spiritual freedom...walking into the sun, breathing deeply, and saying, "Yes I am. I am me today and I have dreams, which can and will come true." A year from now I will live for me, and I will care for me. Today is the day. Stepping into the Jungle

Ask Yourself:

What would trusting yourself look like? How much more confident would you be?

What does making a mistake do for you? Do you withdraw, make excuses, feel stupid?

Is there a way for you to turn a mistake into a valuable lesson? Think of one example.

What are you willing to forgive in others? What will it take for you to let go of past hurts, betrayals and indiscretions?

What are you willing to forgive in yourself? What do you need to do to show some compassion for yourself?

"If I am not for myself, who will be for me?"—Martin Buber

CHAPTER 8
Become Your Own Best Friend

"Progress is impossible without change, and those who cannot change their minds cannot change anything."—George Bernard Shaw

If you can be your own worst enemy, you can also be your own best friend. Embrace change. You are more wonderful than you can possibly imagine.

Are You Ready to Change Your Life?

As far back as the 19th century when self-improvement began to take hold with the work of Ralph Waldo Emerson, the idea of changing your language so you could change your life was an important concept. We can go further back to Ben Franklin to find precedent for this way of thinking. Franklin was considered the granddaddy of personal development but it was in the 1920's that Dale Carnegie created his *How to Win Friends and Influence People* as an antidote to the worry and fear. Even today, it is still one of the most popular self-help books on the market. Writers like Napoleon Hill, Robert Collier, Raymond Holliwell, Dale Carnegie, Vernon Howard and Dr.

Wayne Dyer have all been influenced by this groundbreaking book. Recently, Dr. Barbara Fredrickson said the key to all lasting change is learning how to speak to yourself positively. "Whether you experience positivity or not depends on how you think… Positive emotions – like all emotions – arise from how you interpret events and ideas as they unfold."

People and influences condition us all in our life. It starts with how people spoke to us as children, and as adults many of us are still using the same negative input to run our lives. The language we frequently use on ourselves is abrasive, insulting and self-effacing. We are our own worst enemies, and we can learn how to be our own best friend. Breaking out of this habit is the change we need to make to truly become our best self now.

Growing up, I was taught that life was hard, we should not expect much, and security and love were wishful thinking. You can imagine the impact that had on my life. Flash forward a few years I became determined to find out if that was true and changed my thinking to believe I could create whatever life I chose. I could choose to embrace the positive over the negative, because both cannot occupy the same space at the same time.

You are a 100% responsible for every thought, emotion, action and result you create in your life. When you don't accept this, you are shifting your power to someone else.

You don't need other people to confirm how good you are, how well your life is going, or what you're capable of being and becoming. If I tell myself enough times that I'm doing great, I begin to believe my own story. You are resetting your brain.

When you place too much emphasis on what other people think or are concerned about how others perceive you, you can't see yourself clearly at all. You've created too many stories around who you are and what you're capable of, and what you bring to the world, to be able to see it clearly.

So start by observing how you think about yourself. When you catch yourself thinking something in the negative, write it down. For the next week, write down each time you catch yourself with a negative thought. You'll be amazed at how often in a day that happens.

But if you can think negatively, you can also think positively. Both are on the same coin.

Every time you catch yourself with a negative thought, stop the chatter by rephrasing it in a more positive manner.

Example:
"You can't do that because you don't have the right training."

"What will it take for me to get the training I need to do what I need to do?"

You need to start becoming more conscious so you can choose the life you want wisely. The more conscious you can become, the better life gets. You really can re-program your brain to filter out the negative, the rubbish, and put in the good stuff. It's a lot like having a cupboard full of old food stuffs. The expiration date was months or years ago, and it's taking up a lot of space. Our old stories are like that. They expired a long time ago. We need to throw them out and make room for new stuff to enter.

When we choose our stories we choose our life.

So, I'm here to challenge you. You've gone through however many years of living and you've built up a solid library of stories that run your life. You can make all the excuses in the world for why you're not doing what you could be doing, what you don't do, what you can't do, and what you'd like to do if only….. But I'm here to tell you…

There are No More Excuses… We all make choices.

If the choice you made is the wrong one, then change it again. None of us have to be locked into the place of *Now And Forever*. If that were true, then life would certainly not be worth living. I, for one, do not want to be the lassie fae Leith whose mother was urged to put me into the factory beside her so that I could learn to put labels on whisky bottles. That's a story I didn't want to buy into, and made a conscious choice not to.

We have all made choices that were the wrong ones. We've hurt ourselves, we've hurt others, and we've limited the expression of our true selves for many, many reasons. But you have a choice to recreate, to redo, to explore, have an adventure, move beyond the suffocating and limiting places that you feel locked into. We all have choices. Many of them are unconscious, but many of them are based on the reality of the moment. And if you don't like the reality, then change it.

When people say to me 'But it's ALWAYS been that way' I tell them there is no such thing as ALWAYS. There is only *Until Today*.

Until today I have done it this way, but from this moment, I can choose to do it differently. You can choose to do things differently. It's your life. We give so much of our lives away to others, and the result is we usually feel used up. Women in particular suffer from this syndrome. I'm not saying that we can't be of service to others. That's a whole other issue. What I'm saying is we can't afford not to take care of ourselves. It is counterproductive to living a good life.

I haven't heard a single person tell me they didn't want a good life. We all want better relationships with our significant others, a better job, more money, more free time, more vacations, a better body etc. It's hard wired into us.

So what stops us from getting there? Our stories. The things we tell ourselves and allow other people to tell us.

Try this exercise. It might scare the living daylights out of you to begin with, but do it anyway. Say out loud in front of dozens of strangers that I AM SMART AND GOOD LOOKING, AND I DESERVE TO HAVE THE LIFE OF MY DREAMS.

Okay, so you can't do that, then paste that phrase where you can see it every day. Use it as a screensaver. Remind yourself of that simple phrase and start to believe it is true. It's true because you told yourself it was. You're creating a new story. You're changing the language of how you speak to yourself and you're making choices that are good for you. Don't let other people decide who you are. Decide for yourself.

What's in the past is gone, what's here today is the beginning of the rest of your life. It's a cliché, I know, but it's a very true saying. You have the rest of your life to create the life you want.

Do YOU really want to continue making excuses for why you are not living the life you want?

"We fear beginnings; we fear endings; we fear changing; we fear staying stuck; we fear success; we fear failure. we fear living and we fear dying. We need to push through out fears in order to live a life that matters."—Susan Jeffers

Develop Compassion

One of the greatest gifts we can give ourselves is compassion. The deep caring for self is the secret to lasting change.

I've spent a lot of time talking about getting beyond the mistakes, getting to know you better, and trusting yourself. The process of change is slow but if we stick to it, we can achieve remarkable results in our life. Along the way, we need to develop compassion. We need to learn how to be kind to ourselves.

When confronted with a suffering person in our lives, we have a choice. Most of us will respond with an attempt to do something to alleviate that person's misery, even if it's just to give some spare change to a homeless person. We are touched by the suffering of others, and wish in our heart we could do something more, but frequently do not. For ourselves, we need to nurture that same sensibility. We need to move ourselves to tears when we consider how unfairly we're treating ourselves. We need to move ourselves to action when we see that things could be different if only we took a few extra minutes a day to give more freely with our time and our money, but most importantly, with our heart. Because making change is a heart job. It is about making the connection between your head and your heart so that the heart feels listened to, feels seen, feels needed and nurtured. When we are kind to ourselves, the heart sings. We honor and respect who we are.

Change is an opportunity to be kind to YOU.

You don't have to be Mother Theresa, and you don't have to be saving the planet, the whales, the polar bears or the Amazon. You simply have to save yourself. That is the greatest gift you can give the world. When one person takes good care of self with love and compassion, and above all else forgiveness, you have just made room for the rest of the people in your life to find their own way to that space by being more loving, more generous, more forgiving and more open to them because you are all of that to you.

Happiness is a result of this deep, caring nature. Eckhart Tolle says "the primary cause of unhappiness is never the situation but your thoughts about it. Be aware of the thoughts you are thinking."

You may be holding tremendous guilt for situations that have gone. The stories of your existence have enormous power, but it is your ability to step beyond these stories, to step away from the feelings of remorse and wrongdoing that keep you trapped inside a feeling of self-loathing, that are stopping you from finding the compassion to forgive.

Self-blame and self-hatred are destroyers of life. Learning how to let go of these emotions is the key to developing compassion. They serve no purpose except to keep you in perpetual flagellation of self. Just like the monks of a previous century, in order to prove to the church that they were worthy, we beat ourselves up trying to prove that we are worthy of someone's love and compassion.

The Dalai Lama says "Within all beings is the seed of perfection. However, compassion is required in order to activate the seed which is inherent in our hearts and minds.

Being kind to YOU as well as to others is the highest good we can do.

> *"My religion is very simple. My religion is kindness."*—The Dalai Lama

Forgive Yourself

Learning how to forgive is in tandem with developing compassion.

Growing up I absorbed a great deal of hatred, violence and chaos. I carried that with me into my own life, creating the same kind of mess in the relationships I had with others, with my children, and with my partners. Forgiveness was not uppermost on my mind for the people who had victimized me. I hated my mother and father for all the things they could have done, should have done and didn't do. I was a victim, and I chose to be in victim-mode for many years, which helped me explain my drug and alcohol abuse. It was only when I stepped out of being a victim that I realized the frailty of their existence, and the terrible pain, anger and frustration that they had experienced as human beings living their tragic lives. But I had to write a book before I truly was able to embrace forgiveness as a powerful way to move beyond the stories of my past.

When we hang onto our stories, we hang onto our victimhood. We hang onto the millions of excuses we conjure up each day to justify our existence. This affects the way we choose to live and compassion and forgiveness are a foreign country.

You may be thinking as you read this, "Why would I want to forgive….(fill in the blanks). I'm the one who was hurt by them." But the sad fact of the matter is you continue to punish yourself by holding that attitude. You suffer. The other person has moved on, and may not even be conscious of what they have done to you. You can shake your fist in their face all you want, and perhaps they will be contrite, but that won't resolve the hardness in your heart, or the hurt in your head. Only you can soften this by letting it go.

These are the stories of our life, and they have molded you into who you are now, but you have a choice. You can choose to step away from these stories and you can create your own. I like to say we are either writing our own story or we are living in an epic novel full of the struggles of past generations all vying for our attention in the now. Once more, you get to choose what you want.

Dr. Martin Luther King said " It's our spiritual assignment to love even those who have transgressed against us: for in the ultimate scheme of things, they are learning too.

No one says it's easy to forgive. On the contrary, it can be very hard. But when you succeed, the incredible release you will feel from the burden of holding emotional energy that serves no purpose but to keep you in limitation, is absolute. We have centuries of wisdom telling us how important it is. Nothing, and I mean nothing, is worth holding onto if it diminishes who you are.

Find whatever practice you can to let go of the hurt, pain and torment that dominates your thinking. Recognize that you have within you the power to let go. It is the first place to start.

Tales From The Trail
"People Pleaser No More"—Cookie Tuminello

As women we all struggle with being people pleasers, but as Southern women, your worth is measured by it. I think it's a gene we get at birth. Add to that my full-blooded Italian, Catholic roots and you have a 'gotta feel guilty to feel good' double whammy.

Don't get me wrong, I'm very proud of my heritage. However, because I was taught to be a nurturer and server from birth, it took me a lot longer (50 years to be exact) to figure out what I wanted and where I was going.

Like many Italian girls, I married early (at age 19). Two children and 11 years later, I was divorced, dazed, and feeling like a failure. With a family to support, I got a job and started over. Five years later, I met and married the man of my dreams. After only 14 months of wedded bliss, I unexpectedly became a young widow at 36. Even though I was numb with grief, giving up was not an option.

After several attempts to find my place, I started my own image consulting business, but many years of burying myself in my work and family took it's toll, and I began to question a lot of things in my life. A friend suggested I attend a personal development workshop with her. It would truly change my life. The defining moment was when the coach asked me to stop and check in—I thought he meant the hotel! I had no idea I'd been living my life so cluelessly and unconsciously. I finally got "it" and "it" was three powerful revelations:

◊   *I had choices.*

◊   *I had to please myself first before I could please others.*

◊   *I had to take back my power.*

As a result of these amazing revelations, I climbed out of the people-pleasing hole I had dug for myself. I became a coach and started my own company at 50. Some of us take a little longer than others to get "it."

After I took that first big step, I thought, 'Okay, now what?'

Once you make the choice to climb out of that deep, dark hole of people pleasing, the universe is going to challenge you every day to see if you're really serious. Even though I was considered a gutsy Southern lady, people pleasing had diminished me. It had squelched my passion, power, purpose, and my dreams. Most importantly, it had taken away my precious freedom.

The time had come for me to reclaim the pieces of myself that I'd given away throughout my life. It was time to take back my power and identify the "it" that was holding me back. "It" was…

◊   I was afraid to ask for what I wanted.

◊   I was afraid to say "No."

◊   I was afraid to set boundaries.

◊   I was afraid to charge more for my services.

And what was causing so much fear?

I had to risk not being liked.

When I started my coaching business someone suggested that I use my given name, Beverly, because it sounded more professional than Cookie. Of course, believing others knew more than I did, I agreed. After about a year, I was having a major identity crisis with my new name. "Cookie" had been my nickname since birth, and I liked it. I decided, to face my fears and risk not being liked, and Cookie Tuminello, Success Coach, was born.

The good news about climbing out of the people-pleasing hole and up the ladder of success is that the more you apply what you learn, the more you grow and the more confident you become. Thus I learned that the difference between success and merely surviving was the ability to discover and recognize my own core values, then integrate them into every aspect of my personal and professional life.

Remember my first three revelations? Well, this brings me to my fourth revelation:

Owning The Power Within.

What a revelation it was when I realized that I had all the tools I needed to be successful right inside of me—I just needed to learn how to use them. Again, I thought that was a gene I didn't get at birth.

The Buddhists have a saying, "In the beginner's mind there are many possibilities, in the expert's mind there are few." The idea behind this philosophy is that in order to make changes in your life, you must first empty your mind of old beliefs so that you can make room for new possibilities.

Each year I start off with a theme and a commitment declaration which keeps me on track and honors my intentions. You notice I said commitment. For me, the big difference between setting a goal and being committed to something is that commitment comes from within and goals are the action steps that get you there. In order to fulfill my commitment to myself, I had to be willing to submit myself to the process of change and get support. Yes, coaches have coaches. I don't ask my clients to go anywhere I haven't been or am not willing to go.

One thing I know for sure: if you begin to change the present, the future will surely be different. Stepping off into the abyss can be scary, but the rewards are well worth the risk. Why settle for half a life when you can have a full one filled with passion, purpose, and prosperity beyond your wildest dreams? When you finally realize this, your life will change for the better too.

Stepping into the Jungle

Ask Yourself:

How much negativity do you think is operating in your life? On a scale of 1-10, what does that look like?

What would it take to turn that towards the positive? How much positivity can you stand?

Do you call yourself stupid, useless, inexperienced, fat, lazy (you get the picture)? Give some examples of the negative voices you hear?

Do you think this is helpful? If not, what would it take for you to commit to changing the channel to something more positive?

If you can be your own worst enemy, how can you be your own best friend? What action will you take to be kind, compassionate and generous with yourself?

Notes

CHAPTER 9
Tell the Truth

"What happens when one woman tells the truth about her life? The world will split apart."—Muriel Rukeyser

Radical honesty means having the courage to be who you want to be, live how you want to live, and surround yourself with people who love you for you who are.

What Lies Do You Tell Yourself?

I began to ask myself: What happens when I tell the truth about myself? What will success feel like? What if I'm far more intelligent than I give myself credit for? What if I make loads of money? What if I took total responsibility for my life? What if I can't blame anyone else for the things that are wrong? What if I discover just how magnificent I truly am?

Because of my insecurity, these questions were hard to ask. Perhaps I really was incompetent, worthless, stupid, crazy, useless, and would never amount to much. After hearing it so many times, being given no reason to believe otherwise, it became part of my belief system. The circumstances of my life continued to align with these beliefs. Chaos and destruction followed me everywhere. In my desire to manage my fears, I created the illusion that when things were perfect, all would be fine. If I could control every single element of my life, I would be safe. If I could limit my expectations, abandon any hopes for the future, I would not ever have to be disappointed. If I refuse to speak up, even when wronged, then I would be safe. No one will have the opportunity to reject, condemn, or abandon me, because I have already done it myself. In this tragic overview, I am a frightened child who has become a terrified and lost adult.

Eventually, I was squashing more than I was expressing, and I couldn't carry on that way. It is absolutely exhausting to live like that. The only choice I had was to take the time to see who I was, and reinvent my whole existence—who I thought I was, what I thought I could do, where my life was going. I had to change.

My head told me I could never be successful. I wasn't smart. I would always be poor. But these were the lies I told myself to keep myself safe. It would stop me from being disappointed, from failing should my expectations not be met. These were the beliefs I had assumed were mine because it seemed to fit. I did not see my life as successful. In fact, with a long string of failures behind me in my family and relationships, I didn't see much worth celebrating.

But I was wrong.

As you begin to shift your attention away from insecurity, fears, anxieties, doubts, and shame, you will see a completely different person emerge. As I observed my behavior, I realized

I wasn't a victim, I wasn't being picked on, I wasn't the bad guy, I wasn't a useless failure or a bad mother, nor a terrible, manipulative, and controlling wife—I was just afraid.

Circumstances will never be perfect. If you feel there will never be enough time, money, people, support, opportunities, then this is how your life will remain. Once you accept that you can create the life you want, that it is within your reach, you realize that whatever is offered is a gift not to be refused. There is plenty of everything if you are open to it. No more excuses, it is time to grab for the life you deserve.

Examine Your Motives

Waiting for circumstances to be perfect is a mistake you can't afford. Waiting for the tomorrow that never comes, you are wasting today fantasizing about the future. Another trap is bemoaning the relationships and opportunities of times gone by. When you are tied up in the past, you get bogged down in the present, and you refuse the future. There may have actually been good old days, but chances are they are being viewed through the shade of rose-colored glasses that make them look better than they actually were.

The word happiness doesn't come up immediately in conversation, yet it is the main purpose of existence. People seek contentment, reach for joy, and yearn for peace—but few attain this state. Why? It is my belief that people are conditioned to be *un*happy—conditioned by other people's opinions about who they are, and what they are capable of bringing to the world. Many buy into those opinions because they have been buried deep in their unconscious by parents, teachers, and other respected authority figures. Few get the opportunity to be raised with positive, healthy statements and strong role modeling. And with no role models to follow, the path can be very devious indeed.

Releasing the limiting and stifling definition of who you are is a challenging task. Your identity has been passed on to you by family, experiences and society, and it is deeply influential in how you view yourself. This process of redefining you is the challenge you must face in order to reach your highest potential. This is the journey through the jungle—finding a different path, sharing new experiences, and delighting in fresh discoveries.

As you take these risks you invite more challenges and opportunities into your life. You also acknowledge regrets and begin to forgive yourself for the transgressions of the past. When you admit you are not the perfect superwoman, supermom, superwife, when you give yourself room to be human, you find compassion and forgiveness. Your list of accomplishments is no longer the only measure of your values—the vision you hold for your continued growth instills a fresh optimism and confidence.

Realize that your new schedule must include self-care and an attempt at balance. You must commit to a new set of priorities—setting aside time for solitude, time with friends, outlets for creativity, fitness, sleep, for reading, and for travel. Only by devoting nurturing energy to yourself, will you be able to heal and grow in the direction you choose.

Self-care focuses on sorting out what you don't want, and then what you do want. No longer do you want to do it all, because truly, you can't afford to. You can't afford to give away any more of yourself if it does not serve your needs. The only thing this creates is complete exhaustion and an unrealistic expectation about what one woman can really accomplish. News anchor Jane Pauley left NBC news after twenty-seven years. She was fifty-two years old. When asked why she was leaving, she wisely shared that she was ready for "a life audit." Isn't that a perfect term for this time of life? It was her time to reappraise what she was doing and ask the big question, "What do I really want for the rest of my life?"

When auditing life, you frequently come up short. The question then becomes, "Is it possible to create balance between work and play?" The answer to that depends on what you want; and not just what you want, but what you want enough to create that balance or not. I am passionate about my work at this point, and I know I spend way too much time on it, and allow some of the pleasures like going to the movies or a museum go by. So my audit is not about balance, but whether I'm truly living my life purpose, and at this point, I am.

Ask For What You Want

I had taken care of my children, my husband, done the PTA, community volunteering, made myself available to fill everyone's needs. Now, I wanted a career. I used the expression, "I paid at the office," several times, and now it was my turn. It was time to change the rules in our family. I told my girls I didn't want to be a "Mommy Mommy" anymore. That meant I wouldn't be available for pick-ups, drop-offs, or school events unless I felt like it. Dinner would no longer be on the table every single night as I had done most of their lives; from this point forward, I wouldn't necessarily be there every time they needed something. I had my own life to live, and I had waited long enough. Our daughters were both in their teens at this point, and I thought they were ready. They, on the other hand, felt as if they had been kicked out of the nest. "Does that mean you don't want to be my Mommy anymore?" asked the youngest. "No," I said, "I just don't want to do every single Mommy thing anymore. I'll always be your Mommy. That won't change." Years later, she still remembers that day as the one where I abandoned my mother duties. She doesn't realize that nothing much really changed. I still cooked, organized, showed up when I was needed, but it was on my terms. Just announcing that I was a human being who was more than a Mommy label, gave me permission to enjoy the role and not feel trapped by it.

Do you love flying dreams? The ones where you simply lift off the ground and fly as high as you want to, where there are no barriers to your travel? I've had them many times in my life, and they leave me invigorated and excited. I love the freedom, the ability to cross wide-open spaces. I had a dream once that I was on a chair lift that broke. I watched the steel cables and the chair float down toward the mountain in slow motion, as I flew above, watching the wreckage from the safety of the sky. Now, if I was a dream analyst, I'm sure I could find all kinds of metaphoric images to tie into that one. Freeing myself from the past, perhaps. Maybe the wrecked structure was simply a disengagement from the past. The freedom to fly was the power I had finally claimed to control my own destiny. That is the most vivid image of the entire dream. I am no longer a victim wrapped in the destruction of the past.

Everyone needs to learn how to fly—by themselves, with no machinery, with no one else flying for them. You are capable of your own flight. And in this flying, in the setting loose of your powerful constraints, you are reinventing who you are. Reinvention takes courage. It takes a powerful belief in your own ability to rise above the chaos or confusion of your life. You need to be able to step off the cliff and know you will not be dashed on the rocks below. You can control your own fate. Sam Keen, the author of *Fire in the Belly*, said, "Fear is the sharp edge of excitement." I love that expression and wish I had thought it up myself. I have lived on that sharp edge most of my life, but excitement would not have been the first word I came up with.

Everyone can fly above the trees to get another viewpoint. In coaching, we call it the helicopter view. *What does my life look like from above?* You can look back on your childhood, and on your present life. You can move as far as away from it as you want, or you can come down and sit in the present and experience it differently. You can also fly forward into the future and imagine where this path is leading you.

Since chaos was the dominant atmosphere in my family's household, fear was the dominant emotion. With fear being a constant, vigilance was a key to survival. It was hard to know what was coming next, and I needed to know because there were steps to take in reaction to every variable. What kind of mood would my father be in? What level of despair was my mother experiencing over the state of our finances and her husband's drinking? How frantic or frustrated was she in planning what to do with three children who needed her attention? How much more stress was in reaction to my brother's serious special needs? Our mother was simply too tired, overwhelmed, and afraid herself to protect us. My father's rage was particularly volatile around his two oldest children. The helicopter view of my childhood shows a swirling storm of anger, fear, and pain.

Some of you are remarkably fortunate to be able to brush your teeth and get yourselves to work each day. You could say even surviving your lives to this point has been a great success. But don't stop there. Demand all of it—adventure, laughter, struggle, love, and the joy of dreaming wild dreams. Don't just survive.

Be a SURTHRIVOR!

"*Being defeated is often a temporary condition. Giving up is what makes it permanent.*"—Marylyn von Savant

Tales from the Trail
"A Diva Still Standing"—Debbie Stevens

I was twenty-years-old, in love, and I wanted to get married. Even though I barely knew him, I was convinced the past twelve months had been enough shared time to make such a commitment, and he agreed.

It was spring, when all is renewed, reborn, and I was walking blindly into a trap. Within the first week of our marriage, all hell broke loose. He physically demanded I allow room for his other life—his mates. He was making no changes to his way of living and wanted to continue as he had before. Had I known this truth prior to us walking down the aisle I might have thought differently about our marriage.

Hindsight is a wonderful thing.

The arguments were constant, and the abuse that followed was meant to control me. I was confused. How could this be happening? How could he hurt the one who loved him? Nothing made sense, but I continued to abide by our vows, never daring to challenge him, never risking more pain.

He criticized me every chance he had, even while I carried our first child, reprimanding every mistake; his shirts were not pressed correctly; I cooked the wrong meal; nothing I did was good enough. He even blamed me for being an epileptic.

I became a prisoner of my own home, alienating myself from the outside world. The only friends that remained did so with

155

great caution, aware he could lash out at them if the mood struck. He also used their friendship for his own ends when it meant his ticket for a night out. For me, his nights out were a chance for some peace.

He was not who I thought he was, and as I look back, it seems I simply never knew him at all. There was a five-year age difference between us, and a huge disparity in everything from music to clothes to family traditions. As he pushed me more towards his family, I drifted further from my own. His violent outbursts often left evidence on my body, marks that were sometimes difficult to conceal. It was on these occasions that I isolated myself from anyone who cared for me, especially my mother. She was afraid for her daughter and grandchildren and gave us shelter time and time again.

Many times I left, but I missed him too much to see it through, and by the time it reached its peak, our firstborn was ready for preschool, and the other, just walking.

He did everything in his power to punish and rule me, and I knew there would be no escaping without a war. Our fights brought visits from the police, then were dragged through the courts. I had a restraining order against him, but that didn't stop him. The system is powerless against someone so determined to win, and soon my children and I were forced into hiding.

My options were limited, because not many people were willing to risk his nasty behavior or his threats. It meant we had to go where he would never even think to look. This move would protect my mother, as he would have no need to bother her once the children and I were gone. He soon stopped following my parents, and for a few months, we had air to breathe, long enough to relocate and start again.

We were settling into our interim home when my friend's brother complained about the phone line being dead. Not one person in the house gave it a second thought. On the morning we were leaving for our own new home, I was still in my nightgown, the children just getting out of bed. I waved to our hero who was heading off to the local phone box since the phone was still down and he needed to call his job. The events that followed still seem surreal.

As I turned to get dressed, I heard an tremendous thud. My first thought was that there had been a car accident right outside our door. I rushed to see what had happened, and was horrified to find my friend lying in the middle of the road, neighbors gathered around the scene, and talked of a man in a car.

Someone shouted for an ambulance, and another was saying he'd gotten the licence plate number and sprayed it onto his own car. While all the voices spoke around me, my world fell silent as my eyes fixed upon the numbers staring back at me. "That's my husband's car," were the only words I could speak, and then I collapsed onto the ground. A woman grabbed me and picked me up. She reminded me I was still wearing my nightgown, and handed me a jacket. My body shook uncontrollably. *This could not be happening.*

Between hospital visits and police reports, my children and I set up our new home, but the war with my ex-husband wasn't over. The police had a hard time tracking him down, even though he followed us all day and not once did I spot him.

He returned to our house, hid, and waited our return, when he barricaded us in our new home. We became his hostages for the next fifteen hours, until he surrendered to the police. He went to jail and we were safe, but for a long time I found myself looking over my shoulder. We occasionally received threats that he passed along through his family members, but we survived. Years later, he lost his life to cancer and, finding forgiveness through my faith, my heart grieved for a love gone terribly wrong.

My second marriage has given me back trust in love, proof of happiness, and another child. All the dreams I never thought possible have come true. There is never a negative word, no pain from his hands, only tenderness. I am blessed.

Through it all, I am still standing. I am, after all, a diva.

"Don't let yesterday use up too much of today."—Erma Phillips

Stepping into the Jungle

Ask Yourself:

What would it look like if you told the truth about who you are to yourself, to your family, to your friends?

What would happen if you were to say what you mean, and mean what you say?

Do your failures feel like defeats? What would happen if you chose to use the word "Next" every time something didn't work out the way you expected?

If you want everything to be perfect, why? What would it look like to live an imperfect life, be an imperfect self?

Do you get depressed because your expectations are not met? What can you do to change your expectations?

Do you blame the past for who you are today? Are you a victim or a Surthrivor?

Can you ask for what you want? Would does that look like?

If you spoke your truth, what would it look like?

Notes

CHAPTER 10
Be Responsible for YOU

"The more responsibilities people assume, the more likely they will rise up to meet them."—American Proverb

Taking responsibility for our lives is stepping away from the blame factor.

Refuse to Blame

It is easy to say it is someone else's fault. How convenient to talk about what *they* did to you, rather than accept that you were often a willing participant in the situation.

I used to blame my husband for all the reasons our relationship was not working. It was his work, his attitude, his control issues. He was to blame for all the hardships we encountered. I was just being dragged along for the ride unwillingly and I wanted out. We had been fighting for too many years, and although we had children to consider, I was tired of the fight. What I didn't understand at that time was that I was tired of fighting myself. I needed to move beyond the limiting beliefs

I had created about who I was and what I was doing in the world. I had the self-esteem of a gnat.

The day my husband pointed out that I had made a conscious *choice* to be with him was a mind blower. He said that I had understood all the limitations of his life when we met. He was right. I had willingly surrendered to these limitations from the time we met, believing I was on a magnificent adventure with a pirate hippie. But after several years of being the mistress in San Francisco while he spent months at a time in Thailand with his wife, I had had enough. On the day he told me I had chosen to be in that relationship, I began to understand how responsible I was for my own life. There was no one else to blame for whatever was missing. It was one of my biggest AHA! moments.

Taking responsibility for your own life is something most people say they do, but when analyzed, find out they do not. You are your own worst enemy because what you say and what you do are usually very different things. When you find yourself making judgments about your ability, STOP. It isn't truth, it is simply the *lizard brain* at work.

Everyone has a lizard brain—the part of the mind that is on automatic pilot. That brain lazily rests in the sun soaking up the negative ions of your well-preserved ancient messages that say you're no good, you'll never amount to much, you can't, you won't, you shouldn't, you're not capable, not talented, not enough, not, not, not…. This lizard brain is the part of you that is prehistoric. It's unconscious. Do you really want to reside in that space? If you did, you wouldn't be reading this.

If you have seen the film, *The Manchurian Candidate*, you will have seen how the mind can be manipulated for evil. Now, this may have looked farfetched, but the truth is everyone really can control his or her mind. If you are feeding positive messages to your subconscious lizard mind, it will assume this is the way it should be. You see, the unconscious mind is not a judgmental mind. It simply accepts what you give it. It is neither good nor bad. It just is. It's back to the idea of choice again. You have a choice over what you feed your unconscious and subconscious mind through your conscious thinking. If I choose to tell myself that all is well, and I can believe it on the deepest level of my being, then it will be well. At this moment in time, I feel like I'm one of the most blessed people on this planet. I am surrounded by love, inspiration, beauty, and abundance. This is a long way from the messages I received growing up, and a long way from the thinking that dominated the first fifty years of my life. I now believe I can achieve anything I want, I can be anyone I want to be, and I can have whatever it is I want to have. I am a 100% responsible for every event in my life, every choice I make, and every circumstance that I invite in, even when it doesn't look like it.

When I examine things closely enough, I can see me standing squarely in the choice I made to be there. It's an awesome responsibility, but it's also an awesome amount of freedom.

The universe does not conspire against you. YOU conspire against you. You are your own worst enemy, but you can become your own best friend. You have to be ready to do the work needed and clean up the mess. Not only for your sake, but for your children's sake, because everyone hands down all their dirty laundry from generation to generation.

Make Responsible Choices

We all have a Yadda Yadda radio playing in our heads. The negative voices that are the source of most of our fears. It's the part that believes it can save you from harm by telling you things like "you're not smart, stupid, capable, or you should have known better," etc. Frequently, these are the voices of other people. The influences that shaped our growing up. We are imprinted with other people's fears, doubts and anxieties, and we have a hard time defining whose doing the talking until we take the time to consider the source.

The mind is a trickster. It convinces you that things are real, when in fact it's just your imagination on overdrive. We fear the worst, and we create drama in our lives to match our feelings. It justifies our behavior. It quantifies our circumstances. It supports our case, and we buy into it with complete investment because we believe that it is the only way we can explain the miseries of our existence.

If you recognize any of these symptoms, you are living in fear:

◊   Frantic impatience;

◊   Utter exhaustion;

◊   Often misunderstood;

◊   Being self-righteous;

◊   Emotional paralysis;

◊   Deep sense of shame;

◊   Abject defeat;

◊   Spinning out of control;

◊   Very confused;

◊　Completely overwhelmed;

◊　Constantly victimized.

People are invested in staying in their stuck places. It gets them attention when they complain, when they feel circumstances are against them, when they feel people are not giving them what they need. And it gives them an excuse. Like the man who would be a rock climber if only his leg weren't broken, you never have to take risks or work hard if you have a sad enough tale of neglect and bad luck.

When you can no longer see the benefits you are getting from staying in your stuck place, you will make a beginning toward healthier choices.

Choice is always an option. Even when you don't choose, you are choosing.

Next time you hear a negative voice in your head when making a choice, question the source. Ask who is doing the talking. If you can name it, then it's not yours. Decline the limitation or negative self talk and risk the next bad choice.

I had been with my second husband for seven years when he asked if we could have a child together. The idea terrified me. I had made too many mistakes in the past, and had no desire to repeat them. He said he would give me all the support I needed, but I wasn't sure. I had three generations of mothers behind me who told me that having children was a tragedy, not a joy, and in my own life, I perpetuated it after giving the first child up for adoption, and leaving the second with his father. Why would I want to bring another one into the world with the possibility I would leave it behind too? I did not trust myself to do the right thing. I had left a trail of unhappiness that would take years to heal. I didn't want to be responsible for yet one more. But I realized somewhere in the depth of my soul, that there was a lesson here to be learned. I had to step away from the past and move towards a brighter future. So I did what Susan Jeffers recommended. Feel the fear and do it anyway. I made a decision that my daughter would leave me before I left her, and I worked diligently on my own stuff so that it would become a reality. Thank God, I succeeded. She's now twenty-one and graduating college. I made the right choice, and went on to have one more child, as well as a step-daughter and healed the wounds with my son. My greatest achievement in life has been as a mother.

There are no guarantees in life, except one. Things change. If we are not growing, we are dying. Feed yourself the right ingredients so you can grow healthy and strong.

Being Fearless is not the absence of fear, but the choices and decisions we make when fear shows up in our life.

Love Who You Are

Taking an honest look at your life, you can see that your choices have been influenced by fear much more often than ambition for good results or your true desires. In fact, when analyzing your own life, you may see a pattern of fear that will amaze you. My clients insist that uncovering this pattern is essential to changing their ways. As one client told me recently, "I'm afraid to really be who I want to be because I will hurt someone, or fail them in some way. I say yes when I mean no, and I get so mad at myself and hate them for putting me in this place. I know that all I need to do is stop considering them first, and put me up there, but it's hard."

It is hard, but you must start to put yourself first. Making that commitment to change what isn't working is the greatest gift you can give yourself. By learning how to love yourself, you allow others to love you more and allow them to figure things out for themselves. You can't fix anyone, nor should you try. It's hard enough changing yourself, without trying to change or fix someone else. When I eventually woke up to the fact that anything that went wrong in my very long marriage was not always my fault, I felt very liberated. I reached a place where I could say to my husband with absolute conviction, "This is not about me, this is about you," and he would accept that possibility.

As long as you make yourself the culprit you are not showing self-love and you are not allowing the other person to take responsibility for their part in the drama.

When you stop looking outside yourself for validation, for acceptance, for healing and fulfillment, you will find the love you are looking for. You will find others gravitating toward you because you feel whole, complete, and at peace with yourself. Nothing attracts like someone who seems to be content with life.

The people you surround yourself with are a reflection of who you are. If you are unhappy with someone, or blame them for whatever reasons, it is generally because they mirror some of the negative things you see in your own life. You can blame them if you want, but ultimately relationships are there to teach you who you are, and you must take responsibility for your part in it, including ones that are abusive.

After twenty-nine years in a relationship, it hasn't always been easy to admit that I am seeing myself in his behavior and vice-versa. You always have a choice. Even if it looks like you will lose everything by letting a relationship go, you are actually showing enormous self-love when you make those decisions.

Learning how to love your Self is what taking the fear out of life is all about because love is the opposite of fear. When I can honestly say, "I love me," then I'm accepting who I am in the world, what I bring to the relationship, and there is nothing for me to fear.

People often live their lives through the prism of other people's opinions and expectations, and frequently it is the wrong perspective. They cling to relationships that bring pain and suffering because they are afraid of being abandoned. They see what they want to see, hear what they want to hear, and at all times it is a false illusion about who they are that gets in the way.

If you could see yourself as others do, you would learn to be kinder to 'yourself' and have more compassion for 'yourself', and be a lot clearer about who you are. Learning how to see YOU is the journey everyone is on.

At this point in my life, I know my strengths, my weaknesses, my likes and dislikes. I have learned to honor them and I have learned how to love what I am. I am not a perfect person, and I have no desire to be one, but in my relationship, I do try to understand what's mine and what's his, so we can both live a life that is free from the doubts, anxieties, fears, pleasing, and approval that is so much a part of any relationship.

When you separate from *out there* to *in here*, it may feel there is nothing but emptiness. That's because your focus has been entirely on something *over there*. When you start to take the baby steps toward teaching yourself what it is you want, you begin to see you are not empty; the potential for abundance is magnificent. You are magnificent. If you can be your own worst enemy, you can also be your own best friend by finding out what it is that makes you happy, what makes you whole.

"It is not the end of the physical body that should worry you. Rather, your concern must be to live while you're alive—to release your inner self from the spiritual death that comes with living behind a façade designed to conform to external definitions of who and what you are."—Elizabeth Kubler Ross.

Stepping into the Jungle

Ask Yourself:

What are you willing to do to take full responsibility for your life? Where is there no more blame?

What would you life look like when making better choices? Who would you be? What would you do? Where would you live? Etc.

If you are feeling 'stuck' what investment do you have in staying 'stuck'? How could you do it differently?

Where do you say YES when you mean NO? Where do you use Maybe when you mean NO?

What would it feel like to use your NO more often? What are the benefits of using NO more often?

Knowing what you know, Who do you think you are and Who would you like to be?

"Too many people overvalue what they are not and undervalue what they are."—Malcolm Forbes (1919-1990)

Notes

PART 3
ARRIVE AT THE CLEARING

Notes

CHAPTER 11
Identify Your Strengths

"You need only claim the events of your life to make yourself yours. When you truly possess all you have been and done, which may take some time, you are fierce with reality."—Florida Scott Maxwell

Knowing who you are and what matters to you is what makes your life valuable.

Identify Your Values

I believe that we are all here in this world for a purpose. Everything that happens to us, both positive and negative, is the result of our search for that purpose. But we can't define that until we define who we are. That's why we must drill down deep to find out what are the most meaningful aspects of our life. Find out what are the most important aspects of our life, and what gives us the deepest satisfaction.

In my life, I discovered my highest values were authenticity (what you see is what you get and I try to make it good), integrity (if I say I'm going to do something, then I do it, and I do so with absolute trust in the process), courage (I've learned a thing or two about showing up to the 'stuff') and family (they are the reason I'm doing the work I'm doing. Without them, my life would be a different matter.)

Core values are what define us to the world. Look the following list of words and choose which ones you think describe your personal values. There will be others that I haven't written here, but you get to make your own list.

Authenticity	Generosity	Honesty	Success	Love	Kindness
Loyalty	Community	Courage	Ethics	Creativity	Inspiration
Appreciation	Growth	Good Deeds	Happiness	Wisdom	Warmth
Adventure	Contentment	Knowledge	Wealth	Security	Friendship
Empathy	Service	Good Humor	Devotion	Spirituality	Morality
Good Health	Having Fun	Family	Freedom	Commitment	Open-Mind
Justice	Tolerance	Optimism	Philanthropy	Integrity	Fairness

Of these values, choose four, which you think fits your core values.

These are the traits that are most meaningful to you. The ones you live by. Now ask yourself, how do I live out my core values each day? How do I deny my core values?

Values are what give our life significance. It is a good indicator of whether you are showing up to your fear, doubts and anxieties when we are acting against our best interests. These are the issues that drive us towards our successes in life.

Identify Your Skills and Experience

What are you really good at? We all have a lifetime of experiences that have significantly added value to our lives. The things we have learned along the way about how to be in a relationship, how we in our family and friends are our social skills. Our professional skills include what we had to learn to do the job, how we are in the workplace, what kind of education level have we achieved, and whether or not we continue to add to our educational experience.

Ask yourself what are the most important things to you. Look at the following list and see which ones are the most meaningful to you.

◊ **Accomplishment** - what does that look like and what do you feel still needs to be accomplished.

◊ **Creativity** – how do you fulfill your creative life? What have you done that can be called creative?

◊ **Knowledge** – what have you learned in your lifetime, and what would you like to continue learning, or acquire in the next period of your life.

◊ **Communication** – are you a good communicator? If so, what have you seen is the biggest benefit of that?

◊ **Inventive** – where you do take the initiative and what kind of results do you get?

◊ **Risk-taking** – What risks have you taken in your life and what did you achieve?

◊ **Organization** – Are you well-organized and think systematically? How effective has that been for you?

Other less tangible skills are how dependable are you? How good a team-player are you? Do you have lots of energy and get things done? Are you patient, loyal, helpful, honest, even-handed, good natured, dedicated and competent. Can you be held accountable? Are you flexible? All these and more, are the hallmark of your skills and experience. Everything you've done in your life has led you to develop these and many other traits. So consider what that is for you, and make a list of them. This will determine your strengths and weakness, which in turn you can develop to make them more of what you desire. This you can do by trying new things, experimenting with ideas and attributes that you may not have given much thought to until now. I like to say Be fearless: see where it gets you. It's an amazing thing when you start to believe your capacity for more is in your hands.

Define Who You Are

"Just who do you think you are?"

It's a question usually asked in an angry tone. When I was growing up I heard that question a lot. I was called Madame Muck! Mrs. Stuck Up! Told I was too big for my breeches, (although I never actually wore them, so I can't for the life of me figure out how I was too big for them). Whenever I got cocky or assumed an air of superiority, which was quite regular given the kind of household I grew up in, I was pulled 'back down to size.' Who do you think you are was meant to keep me in place.

And it did. I didn't believe I could be anything more than what the authority figures in my life said I could be. They wanted me small and I obliged.

This was the effect of not knowing who I was. I played small, and it kept me in my place. By keeping ME small, I didn't have to be concerned about how little value they gave me. My response was always to acquiesce and then rebel. My 'F*** U' attitude always seemed to backfire on me because inevitably it was used against ME.

When I gave my first child up for adoption, I had asked for a termination early on in the pregnancy and was refused. The doctor said the world needed babies and I was a strong, healthy girl. Giving her away after delivery proved impossible, and I lived with her for three months before giving her up. It was the hardest thing I'd ever done in my life. It was, honestly, heartbreaking. I didn't know how I would ever recover.

So when I got pregnant again a year later I was determined that I would not go through that again. I marched into the office of the obstetrician to the Royal Family and asked for what I wanted, and expected to get it. Since it was came shortly after a television appearance I made speaking about the effects of unwanted pregnancy and abortion and had named the doctor, he did not refuse this time. I like to think it was because I knew who I was at that moment, and did not accept NO for an answer. Nobody was going to say, "Who do you think you are?" But in reality, I was scared and angry. I was ready for a fight, but he simply said 'tomorrow,' and that was that.

But what if we turn that around? What if I ask you "Who DO you think you are?" and we put a positive spin on that, what do you think would happen?

Now some of you might say, "not much" but if you are truly honest with yourself, you will see, based on the values, skills and experience exercise you did previously, that you have a great deal to offer and who you are is much bigger than you give yourself credit for.

Who do you think you are? You are learning something new here. You are learning how to think differently about yourself as someone with big ideas, big presence, and big ambition. You are learning how to think differently about you.

Your biggest enemy is your mind and the things you tell yourself that you believe to be true. Finding out what the truth really is, that is your biggest risk and your greatest release from fear.

But what if we turn that around? What if I ask you "Who DO you think you are?" and we put a positive spin on that, what do you think would happen?

Now some of you might say, "not much" but if you are truly honest with yourself, you will see, based on the values, skills and experience exercise you did previously, that you have a great deal to offer and who you are is much bigger than you give yourself credit for.

Who do *you* think you are? You are learning something new here. You are learning how to think differently about yourself as someone with big ideas, big presence, and big ambition. You are learning how to think differently about you.
Your biggest enemy is your mind and the things you tell yourself that you believe to be true. Finding out what the truth

really is, that is your biggest risk and your greatest release from fear.

Take advantage of my free study guides at http://www.the-fearlessfactor.com to learn more about how you can start telling yourself the truth.

> *"Trust God, and row away from the rocks."*—Hunter S. Thompson

Tales from the Trail
"The Cheating Husband"—Anonymous

Shortly after getting married in our native South Africa, *he* had voiced his dream of sailing around the world—romantic I thought, but it didn't strike me as my fantasy. It was *his* dream that needed to be fulfilled.

We bought a hull and placed it in the backyard. Every weekend we worked on it, readying it for our journey. But it wasn't real to me. I thought of it as a dream until that first night out at sea three years later. Then it suddenly hit me—My gosh, we really were doing this, and we were so unprepared. It was funny unless you were the one out there. We learned by default, by lessons from nature herself, and by always being pulled forward to the next horizon.

After the carnival in Rio de Janeiro, there were bouts of seasickness on the next leg of the journey—awful seasickness that never stopped. After fifty-four days at sea, we realized I was pregnant! When our first daughter was born, we carried on sailing.

We wandered the world, scratching out a living doing whatever work we could find. We didn't have money, but we were seeing the world. We lived 24/7 together, and between ports, one of us was always awake and responsible for keeping us all alive. When something broke we would repair it as a team. When I became pregnant the second time, we decided to give birth on the boat. After that, all four of us lived on that tiny thirty-four-foot boat, but it was *home*. I had made it cozy with pretty cushions, and everything had its secure place so that, when we rocked at 30-degree angles for days on end, things would stay put.

I am a real homemaker, and enjoyed baking my own bread, preserving the extra fish we caught, and making gourmet meals out of tinned food. There was no refrigerator, no luxuries. The girls' diapers were washed in saltwater, but when it rained I would dash out and give everything a good rinse in the clear fresh rainwater, myself included. I lived with a fear deep in my gut that one of my precious family would fall overboard and drown. The girls grew up knowing that they must never, ever, go out on deck without one of us by their side.

During a stop in San Francisco, we decided to stay put for a while, and my husband got a steady job, traveling to work on ships around the States. We were getting the opportunity to build up the traveling funds a little. Our youngest was still less than a year old, and it seemed a good idea to stick around for a couple of months. And then the letter arrived.

I was not supposed to see it, but it was given to me by a co-worker.

When he came home that night I confronted him, and after some resistance he told me that on the last trip he had moved in with a barmaid he had met...for two weeks.

I begged for an answer.

"Because she was there," he said.

I asked if he was unhappy with our relationship and he said, "No, I love you and I don't really know how it happened, but it did and I couldn't help myself. I can't guarantee that it won't happen again."

My heart broke, and I looked at my world right then and knew I could not walk away—I was a tourist in a strange country with no money. At that moment, I gave acceptance to what I would never have told any woman to accept.

We had both decided we did not want to go back to South Africa to live and so we started the long involved process of trying to immigrate to America. I knew then he would not say the words I so longed to hear, "I am so sorry and I will never do it again."

At that moment I accepted that I would have an unfaithful husband. I began to place little segments of my heart under lock and key, and then we got on with life.

We traveled the world for years, I taught the girls on the boat from correspondence courses and text books, and from observing nature unfold around us. People would always gather on our boat for dinners. Strays always knew they could crash with us until another place was found. We made lots of friends, saw lots of places and nobody knew the dark dirty secret I kept in the bottom of my heart. I didn't enjoy the sailing, but I did enjoy seeing the world and meeting people of other cultures. Shopping in their markets, learning to cook their foods, and trying a hand at their crafts. Outwardly we were the perfect couple.

He continued to travel for his job, and I knew there were women, but I did nothing about it. Later, visits to the gynecologist confirmed that I had contracted a sexually transmitted disease and I had to eventually have a hysterectomy. While I lay in the hospital recovering, another intense affair started—ending with her husband calling me and asking me to call off my "predator husband." She sent me the letters they had both written that she had found. I read them all. I think I hoped to find a key that would unlock it all and give me my life back...the life I dreamed of. When that affair ended, another began and he moved her in to stay with us as she had nowhere to stay. He said she was just a friend—this was all in front of our teenage daughters. After a while, he moved out, then returned, and I accepted him back with open arms.

Why? I don't know.

We decided to sail away to another port, make a fresh start, and I thought life would change. The pattern continued in the new port, until he eventually left for good. I continually wrestled with the questions...where did I go wrong...was I a bad wife?

I finally realized affairs were an addiction for him, and still has. It took a long time before I came to realize that it was not my addiction. I was a co-conspirator though.

Am I angry at myself for staying that long? Not really. I kept that little part of my heart tucked away. When the marriage did break up, it was at a time when I knew I could support myself and two girls going off to college. They both got 100-percent scholarships and are now studying for their doctorates. I could not be more proud of them.

Maybe I still have a little part of my heart that atrophied and went hard after all that time, but now I am in a loving, trusting, monogamous relationship with a caring man. What we go through in life makes us what we are, and we cannot change the past, but we can accept the choices that we made. Sometimes fear of the unknown will keep us in a place for longer than is necessary, but we learn something from each of life's experiences, and in our own time.

The events in our lives need not define us; the way we respond will decide our future.

Stepping into the Jungle

Ask Yourself:

What are your values? What things do you hold sacred above all else?

How do you betray these values in your life by settling for less, or by allowing others to undermine them?

What do you consider your accomplishments?

What are your greatest learning experiences in life?

How creative are you?

How willing are you to take risks to get what you want?

Where are you taking risks right now?

How do you see yourself in one year, three years, five years and twenty years from now?

After defining the above, ask yourself "who do you think you are?" once more.

Notes

CHAPTER 12
Fail Forward

▰▰

"Life always gives us exactly the teacher we need at every oment. This includes every mosquito, every misfortune, every red light, every traffic jam, every obnoxious supervisor (or employee) every illness, every loss, every moment of joy, or depression, every addiction, every piece of garbage, every breath"—Charlotte Joko Beck

In life we are meant to experience the highs and the lows, and in every failure is the gift of trying again.

Mistakes Are A Blessing

This is a time of transition, but it is also a time of transformation. Coming to terms with the past, looking at your successes and your failures, is a necessary step along the way, but it is not where you should linger.

Instead, pursue your dreams, and set goals for your future. Learn that you are indeed capable, that you can and will change the things that make you unhappy, that you can handle whatever life brings your way—that is the challenge and also

189

the reward. There are no more *If only's*. There are only *What if's* and the ability to look toward a positive outcome. Women are a resilient lot. I took a look at the drama and tragedy in the lives of my grandmother and my mother when I wrote *When The Crow Sings*. In it, I also took a survey my own chaotic misadventures, all of which brought great blessings I couldn't see at the time. My powerful future was created by my rocky past.

Personalities are formed at an early age, but they are not set in stone. People change and grow, even morph into something entirely new. You are not the same person you were at the age of twenty, thirty, or forty. Where you stand today is at the doorstep of your own vision to create whatever it is you want to create, to feel secure about who you are and to know you can do anything with desire, determination, and dedication.

Many people are dealing with a potential layoff, going bankrupt, leaving a relationship, elderly parents who are driving them insane, disability, sick relatives, children in trouble, emotional crises. These are real—and very overwhelming. The last thing I mean to do is minimize the effect of these difficult realities. My intention is to help you reach the point where you realize, accept, and declare that you can handle this and any other current problems you face along the way. I guarantee that you are much stronger than you realize.

I've been thrown out on the street with nothing but my bags. I've been denied a relationship with my son, and I've abandoned him. I've seen my house sold for a fraction of what it cost to build and watched my financial life diminish dramatically due to bad investments. I have fought the demons of despair, depression, and helplessness. I've been physically abused, sexually assaulted, and emotionally damaged. Did

I mention I knew a few things about getting past the fears? Been there, done that. The only choice is to carry on fearlessly triumphant.

What's the worst that can happen? You'll die? That wasn't always the worst-case scenario for me; sometimes death was considered a merciful exit from the raw mess my life had become. Perhaps the worst that can happen is that nothing will change and you will live this way for forty more years—ah, now THERE is a death sentence. What's the best that will happen? You'll move beyond all the negatives to find something better and more satisfying. Life is as complicated as you want to make it, and if anyone knows how to do that really well, it's me.

So consider this:

◊ No one is a victim of life unless they choose to be.

◊ *Fear is not the problem. It is only the name you choose to give it.*

◊ When you are helpless, you have given up the ability to choose the outcome of any particular situation.

◊ When you are depressed, it is because you have chosen not to be excited by life.

◊ When you feel you are in paralysis around a given set of circumstances, it is because you have decided to take no action.

◊ *You always have a choice, and even when you don't feel there is a choice, you are making that choice by doing nothing.*

We all make mistakes. It's a normal part of living life. We experiment, we get curious, and we try something new. But when making mistakes becomes an obsession with perfection we are running into trouble. We hold back because we're afraid of making a mistake. We feel vulnerable because we seek the correct answer EVERY time, and we hold back because we think it's not good enough.

Mistakes are lessons to help us get where we want to go. We are failing our way to success by learning what we don't want. This is where mistakes are also our greatest blessing. Why do something the wrong way over and over again, and yet for many of us, that's what we are doing. It's called the 2 x 4 syndrome. A slam up the side of the head until we get it. The school of hard knocks is a hard place to learn, and it's usually because we are afraid to confront our mistakes.

Fear is our belief that we can't handle whatever comes our way. We don't trust ourselves. And the same is true for making mistakes. We don't trust that things will come out the way we want them, and if they don't, that we can choose to do something else. Very few people die as a result of the mistakes we make, which is the worst possible harm we can inflict.

Learning how to admit your vulnerability is a tremendous strength. It is recognition that life is not perfect. We have not reached nirvana where all is equal, so we strive for whatever perfection means in our eyes. Better that we follow the path of imperfection because there is where we learn the greatest lessons.

The Japanese have a name for the art of imperfection. It's called the Wabi-Sabi. It is said that to discover wabi-sabi is to see the singular beauty in something that may at first look decrepit and ugly. Wabi-sabi reminds us that we are all transient beings on this planet – that our bodies, as well as the material world around us, are in the process of returning to dust. It is the impermanence of life and it takes courage to embrace the fragility of it all.

Making mistakes is part of that fragility, and I have only one word that applies. "Next".

When we say "next" to our mistakes, it leaves the door wide open to experiment. When we say "next" to events or circumstances that don't work for us, we have the opportunity to experience so much more than the limited place we inhabited until then. Mistakes are all about expansion. It is your ability to learn something new. Thomas Edison didn't just invent the lightbulb. He tried thousands of things before he finally hit on the right combination to create what he had in mind. I like to say we are failing our way to success.

Failure Means Changing Direction

I was once described by my therapist as a human do-er because I scurried here, there and everywhere trying to make thing perfect, afraid to make a mistake in case I would be found lacking. Control was the order of the day. Everything had a place and everything was on time. I didn't trust people to support me, feeling I would be betrayed or placed in harm's way. I was afraid that if I expressed any vulnerability, I would be abused again. This was my patterning from my childhood. My beliefs were intimately tied up with not wanting to be vulnerable. But it turned out to be the exact opposite. Every time I admitted I couldn't do something, someone stepped up to help. Every time I've made a mistake and admitted it, I've found support and encouragement by the bucketful. But it wasn't always the case.

I hated saying I was wrong. I hated to admit that I was not perfect. This is a one of the hallmarks of someone living their life in fear. Fear is essentially our lack of belief in our ability to handle whatever comes our way. It is a fundamental lack of trust in you.

For years I didn't know how to say I was wrong, because if I did I had to admit I was weak or vulnerable. I made tons of them but they were all exacerbated by my refusal to admit them. I remember one particular fight with my husband. We were in the car en route to a party. He had asked me several days before if I had paid some bills. I lied and said I had because I knew he would be mad at me for not doing it on time. But then we received a second notice, and he was livid. I tried to cover it up with they were wrong, because I was always good at pointing the finger back in the opposite direction, but he wanted to know why I couldn't just admit that I was late with the payment and let it go at that. I insisted I was on time, and stuck to my story. The fight escalated until I was truly the worst human being on the planet. It was all my fault that we had people screaming for money. And still I refused to acknowledge I was wrong.

This is an extreme example, but it was a pattern that I had seen before in my life. The trail of blame and lack of responsibility was a familiar one in my family. No one likes to admit their own failings. They didn't understand the principle of failing our way to success because success was never an expected outcome.

Many boomers are afraid of reaching their 70s with nothing in the bank. We've lived the good life for a long time. We grew up in a time of prosperity. We made a lot of money in the 80s, and even into the 90s, when things began to change. We've earned far more than our parents ever did at younger ages, but we spent more. There is more debt now than ever before. As I write, the housing markets have created a global monetary crisis because so many homeowners are facing foreclosure, mortgages are defaulting, stocks have plummeted, banks are going out of business, and people are struggling to survive after feeling they had it all. Getting out of that takes work, commitment, and, yes, sacrifice. It's clear we can't sustain life as we knew it.

But, oh, do we have the memories. And what wonderful things they are. A friend of mine who indulged in the hippie lifestyle for much of her young adult life joined the work force at age forty-five. When conversation turns to retirement, she takes in stride the fact that she started the game rather late, and says, "Hey. I retired first, and now is my time to work and support myself as long as I can." What a great attitude. She lived her youthful lifestyle to the fullest, and has the rich stories and lessons to hold forever.

Being financially responsible when you get to this age is an imperative. Doris Day was bankrupt at this age because she had left all her financial dealings to her husband. She had to climb back out of her ignorance and pay for it along the way. You can't afford not to be financially responsible now. If you've allowed others to take care of the most important aspect of growing older, you may be financially vulnerable, but you can do something about it. Too many women reach their sixties with nary a clue as to what they are worth, or how to manage things. Every single one of us must assume the responsibility of taking care of our own life. You are capable. You CAN take care of yourself. No one will take care of you unless you give them power over your life, and there are no guarantees that they will always be there. You, however, *will* always be there. Learn how to take care of YOU first.

There's a great book by Liz Perle called *Money, A Memoir: Women, Emotions and Cash*, and is her journey to become fiscally responsible. Suze Orman has made it her life's purpose to educate women on how to take charge of their financial lives. Read her books and get some insight. You need to be more conscious and you can make a difference. She says, "whether we want to admit it or not, each of us has a relationship to money that goes beyond the getting and spending. Money is never just money; it's our proxy for identity and love and hope, and promises made, and perhaps never fulfilled."

I had a coaching client who was deeply in debt due to, as she called it, "Keeping up with the Jones's." She was deathly afraid of how she was going to pay this debt down and continue to live a very modest life in New York City. She and I studied her input and output and looked at where she could go for help. She suggested that her 401K was a good place to start and would talk with her employers. They were very supportive and offered to pay off one of her credit cards, taking the repayment over a period of time instead of paying her matching funds. It was an incredible breakthrough, and it gave her the much-needed stimulus to find other ways to creatively resolve the debt crisis.

Get perspectives on your mistakes. Is it really as bad as you think? Probably not. Can you take the experience and turn it into something else. Change direction, make another decision, be willing to admit you made the mistake, and offer up another solution.

Can you forgive yourself for your mistake? Rarely are they life threatening. If it turned your life upside down, can you recover from it? Was it an embarrassment and nothing more? Move on. For the most part, mistakes are not life threatening, only life limiting if you choose to let them hold you back from saying the one word that will bring out a change of direction.

"Next!"

Learn how to align yourself with success. You are infinitely more accomplished, more capable and more successful than you admit to yourself. Making mistakes means you're growing, expanding in ever-widening circles. When a child falls down, it doesn't think 'stupid me', it gets up and continues exploring her world with a 'no blame' policy.

There Is Power in Failure

When a power grid goes down, they call it a power failure. We lose electricity, the lights go out, and everything goes dark. When we make mistakes, the same thing happens in our mind. We go dark. We presume the worst, and dwell in the negative, until we find the switch that turns everything back on again.

Failure is such a harsh word. "You're a failure", the woman shouts at her husband who just lost his job. "I'm a failure," says the woman who just lost a relationship. "You failed your exam?" a mother says incredulously to her high school daughter. The stigma of failure is profound. We absorb the message into our being, and presume that's what we are. A failure.

How many generals have lost the battle but won the war. We measure our failures by what they represent to us. It is a function of time and perspective that determines how we see the events of our lives. I failed miserably as a mother with my first two children, and I could have stayed there with that thought, but I took a decision to try again, and this time I succeeded. I became a good enough mother to not just the later children, but to ALL my children because I was willing to take another look at these failures to see where I could correct them. And I did. I love all my kids and they are all thriving in life. They understood that my failure in the beginning was simply a result of not having enough information. I didn't know how to be a healthy mother because I never had any lessons in what that looked like.

When we understand the principle that failures are regularly caused by not having enough information, we can then move on. If you are missing parts of the story, then you can't possibly make the right decision, the right choice, take the right direction if you don't have all the information. There is always more we can learn. It is never the end of the story, unless you choose that position. The power inherent in failures is the lessons we learn to make ourselves stronger, more experienced, more alive. That's the true power of the failure.

Success is when we learn how to fail forward. We learn that no matter what comes at us, there is always some other way to look at it. When I lost my house during a particularly challenging part of my life, I was mad as hell. But if I hadn't lost the house, I would not have gone on to live in Europe with my kids for nine years and gave them all kinds of experiences we would never have had.

There is always another way to look at things. You get to choose whether it's a failure or just another choice to be made.

Tales from the Trail
"Singing Without a Choir"—Jacqueline Wales

I was standing on the stage with my mouth dry, my palms sweating and my breath caught in my throat. Eight hundred people at Royce Hall in Los Angeles for Rosh Hashanah services staring at me, waiting for me to open my mouth, and all I could think was, "what are you doing?"

I was about to fall flat on my face in front of all these people, and I would never live it down. In childhood, I had stood in front of thirty people in a church and been so afraid to sing that I ran out the door when it was my turn. I felt the shame of that occasion prickling the back of my neck.

I told myself I had practiced the prayer for months, had developed my singing voice to an acceptable degree, and was well prepared. But it didn't make me feel any better. I felt foolish and inadequate, which wasn't an unusual feeling. I had felt that way most of my life. But I was here, and there was no turning away. I took a tight breath, and the words and music began to flow from my mouth.

The first few notes were strained. I tried not to concentrate on the number of people there, but instead, looked for my husband who was sitting with my daughters in the fourth row. He was smiling with a look of immense pride on his face. The song was L'chi Lach, a prayer from God to acknowledge how much of a blessing we are and can be. I was being blessed right then with this very special occasion, but I was so afraid of forgetting the words, of missing a note, of sounding bad in front of all these people. I could feel the Rabbi and the Cantor behind me, sending me their love as I sang, and as the notes unfolded, I felt my body relax and the sound began to soar. I was caught in the beauty of the moment, in the melody and the pleasure I got from singing. I was in heaven.

The song finished and although it's not the custom to applaud during religious services, I could see the smiles on people's faces, my husband and daughters beaming back at me, and when I turned to walk back to my seat on stage, the Rabbi and the Cantor gave me a kiss on the cheek as I walked by and said 'well done'.

As I sat down my whole body went into a state of tension release, quivering from head to toe. The woman sitting next to me leaned over and said, "you were terrific." I smiled weakly through shivering teeth, aware of the happiness exploding within me. This was a fearless moment, and although singing publicly would still challenge me, there would be many more opportunities to enjoy the thrill.

"Fear is the sharp edge of excitement."—Sam Keen

Stepping into the Jungle

Ask Yourself:

Do you consider yourself a failure? If so, why?

Do you live your life in 'if only's' and feel guilty for past mistakes? What would it take to move beyond them?

Are you willing to forgive yourself and others for their mistakes?

Do you feel you are a victim of life, feeling helpless or hopeless? If so, who do you need to be to change that?

Do you feel vulnerable when you admit your mistakes? What would it look like if you admitted your were wrong? What's the worst thing that could happen?

Are you ready to move beyond your mistakes and see them as simply the learning blocks of your life? What have you learned from your mistakes?

What does failing your way to success mean to you?

Notes

CHAPTER 13
Change Your Language

"It's not what we don't know that gives us trouble, it's what we know that ain't so."—Will Rogers

Learning how to speak the truth of who we are takes courage. Learning to reject the negatives and embrace the positives is our journey.

What Is Conscious Thinking?

Most of us operate out of a mental fog. We walk around on automatic pilot in constant discussion with ourselves about what is good, bad and indifferent. Much of our thinking is in the negative and we evaluate life from the perspective of limited beliefs. Getting conscious is the act of deliberately choosing what we wish to think, making decisions that are based on the reality of the situation we find ourselves in, and constantly seeking the expanded answers to our questions, instead of the automatic pilot messages of a brain that has been programmed towards limitation. We are choosing our thoughts. We are choosing our direction.

Rene Descartes is famous for saying "I think, therefore I am," but the statement is misleading. What we think is not necessarily who we are. What we think is usually a muddled concept of who we 'think' we are.

It is the job of conscious, rational thought to decide what you want, select the goals you wish to achieve, and concentrate on these rather than on what you do not want? This is the power of positive thinking. We have it within our control to take our thoughts to a higher level, but it means staying vigilant to the old patterns of thinking.

As a culture we care about what goes into our bodies, but we are constantly bombarded by toxic thinking that we don't even notice. The messages of self-hate, of disapproval, of dismissal are all around you. When you call yourself stupid, you diminish yourself. When you tell yourself you are incapable of doing something, you have already built a box around yourself. When you have disparaging remarks of any kind against yourself, you are placing yourself into a lowly position that on reflection you would not even engage in with worst enemy. We are a hive of negative thinking buzzing around our heads all day long.

According to a study done by the University of Chicago several years ago, they found that over 70% of our daily thinking is in the negative. Is it any wonder that our world is filled with fear, doubt and anxiety? It is mostly self-created. We are our own worst enemies, and by changing our language, we can become our own best friend. Cutting down on the unhealthy carbs of mind-numbing negativity is the kindness and compassion you show to yourself. This is the start of building the best life now. We start by learning how to speak to ourselves from a conscious place. We choose to be kind, we choose to be positive, we choose to have compassion for whatever it is we think we are. Being fearless is not the absence of fear, but the choices and decisions we make when fear shows up in our lives. That's the secret to overcoming ALL fears. This is the same for our thinking. We must choose to think differently.

In the 90's Apple Computer put out an ad campaign that simply said Think Different. Pictures of Einstein, Gandhi, John Lennon and a host of other independent thinkers graced the ad on television and in the movie theatres. But it was Thomas J. Watson who worked for NCR before it became IBM, who said "Thought has been the father of every advance since time began. 'I didn't think' has cost the world millions of dollars." They used the word 'Think' in their marketing program before Apple, who took it one step further and asked us to Think Different.

We lose when we don't think. In order to grow, to expand, to embrace change, we must Think Differently. If your current way of thinking is not getting you anywhere, doesn't logic tell you it's time to change. But you resist, because changing means your world will change and then where will you be? Think about that? Probably in a better place if you are thinking positively.

George Bernard Shaw said, "progress is impossible without change, and those who cannot change their minds cannot change anything." The wonderful thing about conscious living and conscious thinking is we get to change our minds until we find the right fit for us.

Negatives Are Destructive

I was not born into happy circumstances, and if this is beginning to sound like a Dickens novel, it was. Everything in my life was surrounded by misery. The people I looked to for security and love were unable to give it to me because they did not know how to give it to themselves. They lived the bulk of their life in an unconscious haze. They believed that life was hard, that you were a fool to have expectations because you would always be disappointed, and dreams were a waste of time. Ultimately, you would end up disappointed and in despair. Success was something that happened to someone else.

Well, you can see how much I actually believed that, but it took me a long time to break the habit of expecting bad things to happen because they always did. What you believe is your reality, will manifest in our life. Take a look at that in your own life and see if I'm not right. We create the reality we want, even when it looks like it's all bad stuff, but the interesting part is we can also create the good stuff.

I learned how to dream. I learned how to change my language. And I learned how to change my life.

Changing my language started when I was seventeen and had moved to London from Edinburgh, Scotland. I had a thick accent from my native town, and in 1969, London was in full swing, and the only accent that was acceptable was Cockney. The rest were peasants from the provinces. The BBC English ruled the waves, and plums in the mouth came standard. In order to feel more acceptable in society, I had to change my language from "Ye dinnae ken anything!" to "You don't know what you're talking about!" This was step number one for me. I wanted to feel like I was part of the society I had placed myself in. I wanted to belong and not be a misfit. But I didn't really believe I could do it because the messages in my head said otherwise. I was just "a lassie fae Leith whae hud big dreams in her heed." I was going to get in trouble, just as my mother had predicted, and I did. I was pregnant by the time I was 19 with no immediate claim on a father that I could pinpoint. Too many 'bad girl' nights.

One of the phrases that always struck me as being particularly limiting is "but I've always been that way." It's a now and forever phrase and it indicates that there is no choice. My preference is for the phrase "up until now I've been that way," with the clear indication that you have a choice as to whether you stay there or not.

When you change your language and you become conscious of your thinking, you'll notice a lot of gremlins making noises in your head. These are the voices of 'reason' of 'safety' of 'direction' of 'worry' of 'criticism' of 'judgment'. There are many types of gremlins in your mind, but they all have one thing in common. They think they know what's best for you.

If you stop to think about these voices, who do they remind you of? A parent, a teacher, a boss, your sister, your best friend? Many of us carry the voices of other people around with us because at some point they were the authority figures and we believed what they told us. Our gremlins are the referees of our life. We believe them because they perpetuate the myths that we buy into. The "I should's" or the "I cant's" or "I'll try" with no willingness to go beyond the try stage.

Changing these negative voices is your task if you want to create your best life now. When you hear the words "I can't" in your head, be alert to what is behind that. Is it fear? Worry? Doubt? Anxiety? Guilt? Consider this possibility. Instead of trying to chase the thought out of the way, or giving into it, replace the idea with something else. Reframe the words you just thought. Replace 'can't' with *won't or will, or choose to, or not choose to.* You are reframing it so you do have a choice. You are choosing to think consciously.

Example:
I can't tell him how I feel because he's going to get mad, so I choose not to tell him how I feel because I don't want to experience his reaction. Then you've made a conscious choice about the consequences of this action. You've made a decision to stay out of the argument, at least for the time being.

There is little we can't do if we really want it badly enough. We just have to learn how to move out of our own way.

Learn How To Love Speak

Speaking to yourself with compassion and love takes practice. It also means keeping people who are toxic out of your life. People who poison the air with diminished expectations of who you are. People who humiliate or embarrass you so you behave small and inconsequential. People who bully you or make you feel that your life is not as important as theirs. We have all had people like that in our lives, and the sad truth is that they are doing it because they themselves feel small and insignificant. You don't need that kind of energy around you. It is not up to you to try to change them. Your responsibility is to change yourself, and you cannot do that with toxic people around you.

However, having said that, if you find yourself in a job where your boss is a pig, or you're in a relationship with someone you love, but doesn't get the harm he or she is doing to you, then make a decision that it will have to change. The earth won't crumble, and your life won't end if you choose to be in a healthier relationship, or a healthier work environment. But it will mean that your choices may be hard, and you will have to decide what is more important. Your health, or their insecurity. That's the choice.

Creating your best life means an awareness of choice. When you are not in touch with your choice of words, when you are not in touch with your emotions, when you are not in touch with the joy that is in you when you are not living true to who you are, you are dying inside. You have to ask yourself what for?

I like to say that fear is our passion dying to get out. When we hold back, withdraw or make excuses for thing we don't want to do because we're afraid, we are denying the power within.

When you don't OWN the power that is you, you are not expressing the natural energy within that wants to be seen, to be heard, to be alive and joyful. Learning how to claim that is what learning how to love yourself is all about.

Confronting the demons of your mind, getting conscious about what makes you tick, and being willing to confront the people and situations that are not working is learning how to love who you are. To create a meaningful life, we must step off the cliff and trust that we will land safely on the other side.

When you give up doubting yourself, stop beating yourself up with criticism and judgment, start believing you are capable of handling whatever comes your way, you have chosen to make fear your ally, instead of your enemy. Every time you hear that alarm bell going off, it's the call to wake up and pay attention. There's something here that doesn't fit right with who I am. It's telling you something that doesn't fit with you are.

I'm one of these crazy people who absolutely love change. I've been running all over the world for years because I love the stimulation of change. I feel alive when I'm searching for what's next. I was described by a friend years ago as a Searcher. It's a compliment. I can stand in my Clearing and know that who I am. That's what I invite you to do.

Develop compassion for you. Compassion means to alleviate distress, and you are doing that every time you make a decision to be kind to yourself by not judging, not criticizing, not calling yourself names. If we cared for our own suffering as well as we cared for the suffering of others, the world would be a happier place. We are taught from the earliest age that we must respect others, but many times the message to respect yourself is missing. Compassion is the most meaningful measure of emotional maturity. "It is through compassion that a person achieves the highest peak and deepest reach in his or her search for self-fulfillment." Arthur Jersild.

Along with compassion goes gratitude. This is another way of being kind to yourself. When you live in gratitude for all the gifts in your life, you express your thanks in the small acts of compassion and kindness you perform each day. Compassion and gratitude combat stress.

Each night before you go to sleep, write out the things you're grateful for that day. Only the good things of your day, not the negatives. "Today I am grateful for…" Keep it in the present. Don't write "I was grateful for…" because that means you have allowed the opportunity to pass. Keeping it in the present makes it easier for you to hold that feeling in your body. You don't want to record that you had a lousy fight with your husband, or you screamed at your kids and felt bad afterwards. Be as specific as you can in the details about your gratitude because that will allow you to relive the experience and the happy feeling it will evoke. Don't include any negative statements in your gratitude. Nothing that sounds like, "I'm grateful I didn't get mugged on the way home from the late night movie." Gratitudes don't have to be important. They can be as simple as a smile from a stranger. Gratitudes are also not accomplishments. They are acknowledgments of the state of grace you move through in your daily life, most of which goes unacknowledged. At first, you may not have much to write about, but as you retrain your brain to take in details of the positive life, you will start to notice the things you are grateful for. Being in a state of gratitude brings positive results.

Make a list of all the events in your life that you consider failures and all those you consider successes. You will be surprised at which list is longer. You are much more accomplished than you give yourself credit for. Anyone who has an abundance of fear downplays their success list. Women in particular have a habit of saying, "Anyone would have done it that way," as a manner of explaining something courageous in their life.

You must start noticing what you are doing in your life that creates a positive effect. You are so much stronger than you think you are. It may be the Greek god Atlas of ancient mythology, who holds up the world, but it is women who truly held up the world. Without women, there would be no world, at least none populated by humans. So start taking back some of that power. You deserve it.

Fearless Meditations

Do these affirmations and see what a difference they can make.

◊   I breathe *in* abundance.

◊   I breathe *out* gratitude for all that I am and all I can be.

When you can express your gratitude for all that you have, and for all that you give to others, you are blessed with abundance in life.

◊   I breathe *in* trust.

◊   I breathe *out* expansion of self.

For many, trust is one of the hardest things in the world, but when you learn how to trust, your world opens up into a fuller expression of who you are.

◊   I breathe *in* faith.

◊   I breathe *out* belief that I can create the life I want.

Everyone needs to have faith in the ability to create the life they want. It is within your power to do so.

Choose some affirmations for yourself. Be sure to make them positive. Don't use *I will* statements because you are putting that into the future. Choose a statement that reflects the here and now.

For example, instead of *I will feel less fear in my life*, which is a statement of future possibility, say: *I am now handling my fears*, which is a statement in the present.

Becoming conscious is an act of great vigilance...noticing how you speak to yourself, how you speak to others, and how you make adjustments to old habits. It is time-consuming, can be exhausting, and you may find yourself getting fed-up with the process. Keep in mind that you didn't acquire all these bad habits overnight, and you won't get rid of them quickly either. But the rewards of becoming conscious of who you truly are, are extraordinary. Patience, persistence and determination will change your life.

This is where your health resides, in a positive state of mind about every aspect of who you are. When you change one thing, you are setting up a chain of reaction in every cell in your body. Your whole self is in the process of transition. You can't compart*mentalize* (note the end of that word), because everything is related.

Love yourself and watch other love you more. You can see that when people respond to you about how well you're taking care of yourself. When you care enough to say to someone 'that doesn't work for me' or I have to say no because I choose something else. That's love speak. Treat yourself as your best friend. Nobody knows you better than you do, but you have to give yourself the opportunity to find out who you are.

Tales from the Trail
Envisioning Vickye—Victoria Stephens

I am a workaholic when I am focused. This by itself is not a bad thing, but after so many years of work at my administrative desk job and the co-dependency in my drug-addicted family, I began to dislike waking up and began taking anti-depressants. I had become obsessive, smoked two packs of cigarettes per day, and wasn't paying any attention to myself. I didn't want to think about my life and had become irritable with my staff, often yelling at them. I was having trouble sleeping and was getting up to work on a new spreadsheet or database in the wee hours of the morning, seven days a week. I could feel my mind and body breaking down but couldn't stop myself. At the same time, I was afraid that if I did stop, there wouldn't be anything left to live for.

I took up yoga in an effort to de-stress, and I am so very happy that I had started working on my body and my mind before it all caught up to me.

At fifty-seven, the years of stress and denial had done me in. I needed cerebral vascular surgery to remove a bladder tumor, carotid artery surgery, and cataract surgery in both my eyes. These surgeries and my retirement put me to bed for a year, which turned out to be a much-needed rest. However, the important part of all this is that I had no fear. I felt completely relaxed during all the surgeries. Much of this I attributed to yoga, but making the decisions to stop beating myself up and to retire were both great decisions. I also discovered I had friends. I didn't have to go through all of it alone. My friends stepped forward to support me, and their outpouring of love gave me a wonderful, liberated feeling.

I felt rested, loved, and healthier than I had in years. A dream had come true. My family began to pull themselves together on their own, I was getting healthy again, and I could now do what I wanted. The next year, I began wondering what that might be; I still had no idea what path to go down but now knew that I had so much to live for. My employer had a great retirement program: health insurance, a livable monthly income, and a 403b plan in which I had the foresight to make an investment. My flat was big, inexpensive, and in a city that offered many opportunities. My closets were full and I discovered that I really didn't *need* anything else to make myself comfortable. I was lucky, yet my decisions were difficult; I could go in so many directions that it was hard to choose.

We have all heard that life is what we make it. That phrase may have become a dead trope since, for many, what is not so clear is that one must still be rooted in honesty when envisioning what we want to make of our life. Looking at ourselves—our strengths and weaknesses—honestly and with recognition, is a difficult process that lasts throughout life; it is our karma, so to speak. As it is with many, my strengths are also my weaknesses. But what does that mean? As the poet Shelley said, "... Where is the love, beauty and truth we seek, but in our mind?"

There are many paths to the truth within us and we can each choose which path we wish to follow. One of the paths I chose to follow is what is called "the path of the heart," i.e., the path that sees and recognizes whatever is making us fearful and can then transform that fear into courage. This is one of the paths I have chosen, a path to a future I hadn't seen for many years. Of course I am still working on learning about myself and will for the rest of my life. Strength often lies in experiencing the joy of courage when a fearful truth is known, i.e., when it dawns on us that we are a part of nature with our own unique abilities and can actually handle it. Being human is complex and being a woman can be more complex.

As a woman, I have more of the feminine characteristics of being human, i.e., intuition, nurturing, socializing, etc., than a man naturally would. Sometimes, as women, we lose ourselves in the needs of others and often this loss can make us unconsciously angry or fearful. We let ourselves go, we're afraid of change, we don't appreciate what we do have, we are worried that others would not like who we really are, we don't really like the responsibilities that appear in our lives when we are taking care of someone, or worried about someone. How can we possibly admit the restrictions we placed upon ourselves that led to such a life? It is necessary to be truthful with ourselves.

However, that does not mean we must stop nurturing, or stop socializing, or not pay attention to our intuition. We are woman, hear us roar. We know things. We have our own weapons, face different enemies, and make different friends. It's okay to have limitations and not try to be Wonder Woman all the time. When I learned I did not have to do it all myself, I found there were people who cared about others and who were available. There are many resources, male and female, available right now to help us pull ourselves up out of our fearful state. *Fearlessness is not the absence of fear, it is the courage to face our fears head-on.* It is treating ourselves with love and respect for what we have accomplished and what we will accomplish, and relaxing into the life we have chosen and/or are making.

I no longer do yoga every day, but I am training myself to take long walks and be aware of my surroundings, the noises, the colors, nature. Most of the time, it is all wonderful. I took a trip to Europe for another change of perspective. True, it was expensive, but worth it. I have now moved into my 60s and it is a great time of life. Wisdom begins to flow in from life's experiences and we move to a different drummer. And, while I am still working on my weight, I am still rather pretty. Life, Love, and Light to you all.

"I think the purpose of life is to be useful, to be responsible, to be compassionate. It is above all, to matter, to count, to stand for something, to have made some difference that you lived at all."—Leo Rosten

Stepping into the Jungle

Ask Yourself:

What negative names do you call yourself? How you could speak about yourself differently?

When you get tired, hungry or stressed do you revert to childish behavior? What does that look like?

How is your thinking affecting your health? What could you do differently?

Where do you avoid confrontation because you don't know what to say?

What will it take to turn your language from negativity to positivity?

Can you speak to yourself with compassion and forgiveness? If so, what would that sound like. Be specific.

Are you writing in your gratitude book each night? If not, then when would you like to start?

Practicing meditation is known as a major stress-releaser. Start by practicing the affirmations found in the preceding chapter.

CHAPTER 14
Explore your Passions

^^^

"Nothing great in this world has been accomplished without passion."—Georg Wilhelm Friedrich Hegel

It's hard to get anything meaningful done if you don't believe in all you can be.

What Gets You Out of Bed In The Morning?

You may have spent your life committed to your work, committed to your family, and committed to your way of life. But now you may be reaching a place where you start to wonder what's next. You've heard the expression *follow your passion* and wonder what that means. For some, it's the expectation of some great romantic fling or an overwhelming physical experience. For others, it feels like a foreign country. A place you once longed to visit and somehow lost the map that would lead you there.

Passion can mean losing your head, losing control. It can also mean overwhelming emotions and possibly anger and rage. A passionate murder…lost in a fit of passion. It can also be an experience of following something that you love, that sets your world on fire, and makes you feel as if every day is a gift from God.

While I was growing up, my mother admonished me with, "Don't get carried away." But it was hard, maybe impossible, for me not to. I've always been a passionate individual. I've always wanted to experience life fully, and frequently followed my passions to all the wrong places. My mother lived in fear of her passions. She suffered for them and transferred that fear to me. But when you are passionate, it's not rational. It's pure emotion. You can't explain passion except by the actions it inspires.

Three years ago I started Fearless Fifties, and as I reflected on what my life has been I realized that P.A.S.S.I.O.N was an acronym for the seven stages I went through to make changes in my life, and it applies equally to everyone I've ever spoken with about the nature of change. The seven steps are **Permission, Action, Strength, Support, Inspiration, Owning** (confidence) and **Nurture.**

◊ **Permission**. Step number one was giving myself *Permission* to move beyond the limitations and fears that held me in a negative grip, *Permission* to step away from asking others if it was okay for me to live my life the way I wanted. Permission granted to myself to create whatever I wanted. To take a new direction. To make decisions that were good for me.

◊ **Action**. I had to make a plan, or at least have a sense that whatever I wanted was possible if I would only do things differently. I began to focus on what was true to me. I began to think about what it would take for me to do what I wanted to do. To become who I wanted to become. To write well, I need teachers, to sing well, I need teachers, to become a black belt in karate, I needed teachers. But I also needed commitment and focus, and a stick-to-it attitude that evolved as I made my plans.

◊ **Strength**. When I took action I began to understand my own *Strength*. All my life I had battled the demons of insecurity, lack of self-esteem, depression, and abuse. I began to understand that not everyone makes it through to this other side. Many, like my brother, end up in jail, or, like my father, succumb to the deadly grip of drugs and alcohol. You could say the deck was stacked against my succeeding, but somewhere buried under the dung heap was the belief that there was always something more for me. On reflection, I realized that it took enormous strength of will to overcome many of these obstacles, and that would continue to support me in my forward motion.

◊ **Support**. As I developed my strengths, I searched for *Support* to help me get further along the path. I found therapists, coaches, inspirational speakers, books and tapes to educate myself and learn from the past. Getting support was the key to my success. Without these amazing guides on my journey, I would never have known which path to take.

◊ **Inspiration**. On this journey through my own jungle I received *Inspiration* from all the people I had worked with, and met. As a result, I was hungry for more and began to feel confident about what I was doing.

◊ **Own It**. Developing confidence takes time, and a lot of people who believe in you as you learn how to believe in yourself. I began to *Own* who I was becoming because I could see ME more clearly. I removed the veil of the past and I developed confidence in my skills, my experiences, and my knowledge. I called it standing in my own shoes.

◊ **Nurturing**. I had to learn how to *Nurture* myself. I gave myself permission to do what was good for me, had regular massages, went to visit the chiropractor, and exercised regularly. Stopped drinking, gave up drugs, learned how to speak to me with kindness and compassion, and did this because I realized if I took care of me I could then take care of others more appropriately.

The passion I speak of is the thing that gets you out of bed in the morning. In the best possible circumstances, passion drives your choices around work, money, relationships, and what to do with the rest of your life.

My passion is writing. I can't imagine a day without writing something, even if it's just a note in my gratitude book. I wrote part of this book in Bali while on vacation. It didn't feel like work. In the distance the priests were at the temple in the rice fields, performing their prayers on a loudspeaker for the entire community of villages around us. They had woken me more than once at 4am and 6am. That's their passion. They are blessing the rice fields for the harvest to come. So I wrote to the strains of Balinese prayer, which is a musical sound akin to Jewish cantorial prayers.

For five years I was a High Holidays lay-cantor for synagogues in Paris and Amsterdam. Singing transports me to places far away and takes me to the center of my creativity. I have sung prayers and been lost in the reverie of the music. Passion is the ability to lose yourself in time and space when you are engaged in pursuing things that matter to you. When you are passionate about something, your eyes light up when you discuss it. Your energy is boosted, your attitude is improved, every bit of your attention is absorbed, and you just feel *right*.

The first step to putting PASSION into your life is **Permission**.

We make too many excuses for what we don't do and why we can't do it, and we frequently ask if it's okay for us to be doing something, instead of stepping up and saying, "This is what I need to do. This is what I will do. This is all about me, not you." We apologize for our existence, instead of celebrating it. We don't ask for what we want, until it's too late when we realize we are not getting what we want. So you must give yourself permission to live life on your own terms.

This is not selfish behavior. This is responsible behavior. It's the most positive, empowering thing you can do for yourself. It says loud and clear, I'm Important. You *are* important, and your needs should come first. They say you can't truly love another person until you learn to love yourself. I believe that to be true. I also know that until you start loving yourself, you will never be able to create passion in your life.

Have you ever looked in the mirror and told yourself, "I love you"? Sounds silly, doesn't it? And believe me, you feel pretty stupid doing it the first, second, and third time. But try it. Try saying something similar to, "I like you. You're a cool woman." Or, "This is what I like about you." Have a conversation with yourself in the privacy of your bathroom. Your partner might wonder who you're talking to, but if you're anything like me, you might be used to talking to yourself anyway. In fact, many of you might be in a relationship where talking to yourself is the best option.

You give yourself permission when you can start to dream about what you would like to have in your life and step into the challenge of what it takes to make it happen. When I started my business in 2006, my biggest fear was asking my husband for the money to make it happen. In our household, there was a long power struggle over money. I came into the relationship with none, and although he said, "What's mine is yours," it came with a proviso, "providing you ask first." I never felt that I had any control over it. Whenever I wanted something, he had to know how much and what was I going to do with it. I felt like a servant with cap in hand.

Now, there is no denying this was my issue. Like many people, I have issues around money and my relationship to it, but after twenty-six years of living together, this was something that had to end. I had to give myself permission to step away from the habits of the past and move towards my desires— my passions—and know it was coming from a true, authentic place. I have found that the key words in my life have been *focus* and *determination*. When I am truly focused on what I want, and am determined to get where I want to go, that's the permission I need to give myself.

When I approached my husband for the first time about starting a business, his initial question was, "How much do you need?" This was not a question with an open-ended answer. Couched in his response was, "How much is this going to cost ME?" I dithered, and he said he would think about it. He would think about it—here I was asking permission again. What was I thinking? This was old stuff. When you ask permission, you give someone else veto power over your life. I had no intention of going there, but the old resentments kicked in. How dare I have to ask, how dare he equivocate, how stupid that, after all these years together, I was still asking him if it was okay.

Here I was creating a business around the issues of being *Fearless* and yet, I was asking him if it was okay. I had to shift my perspective and step beyond my fear of rejection. He chewed on it for a month, while I waited. Eventually, on a calm Sunday afternoon, he came into my office and we began a conversation that ended with me telling him exactly how I felt about starting my own business, how I had always asked him for what I wanted, and how that no longer worked for me. It was a turning point for our marriage. We heard each other's concerns, and I felt respected for my opinions. I need to say here and now, my husband is not an unreasonable man. He is a caring, generous spirit, but he has his own issues around money, and this is one of the few places in our relationship that still sticks. He left this conversation with, "I'll think about it."

The following day we met in the bedroom while dressing, and he said, "I've thought about our conversation yesterday, and as your partner, I have no option but to support you in what you want to do." I was delighted to hear this response because he knew this was an open-ended financial commitment. I had no idea how much it was going to cost me to make this happen, but I was willing to take the risk, ready to take charge of my own life. But the phrase he used still stuck.

I said, "How about you take the words 'no option' out of the phrase and we have a deal?" He shook his head and said, "Whatever." It was too much to push for the perfect phraseology, but it was good enough. I went forward with my dreams to create a place where women could explore what it is to be fearless, and help others step into the places where I had been—and continue to go.

Finding your passion is essential to living your best life. I have never worked harder, nor felt so fulfilled as I do at this time. Learning how to give myself what I needed was the key.

Where In Your Life Do You Feel The Most Joy?

Joy is a subjective issue. We find joy in the birth of our children, in the celebrations of marriage, in the things that make us feel good. It is a fleeting emotion for the most part, and we need to consciously focus on it to help it stick around. So what does joy and happiness mean to you. The Dalai Lama says we are all looking for happiness in life. It is the single biggest desire in our experience of life, but it is also the hardest to define, and the most illusive to find.

Some people are happy no matter what is going on in their life. They meet the challenges with an open mind, and an expectation of positive outcome no matter what. They are the optimists of life. We could call them Pollyanna's but they truly believe that life is a good thing, and that all we need to do is shift our perspective. Dr. Martin Seligman, author of Authentic Happiness and Learned Optimism is a positive psychologist. He says "pessimists always have wet weather in their soul." They don't do well at work, are continually sick, and their relationships go sour very easily." He also says we can learn how to be optimists. "People need to recognize the catastrophic things they say to themselves. It's as if they have an external person whose mission in life is to make them miserable. "What we have to do is dispute this thinking in the same way you would an external person. We generally have the skill of disputing other people when they make false accusations, and we can learn to do so with ourselves as well. That's the central skill in learned optimism training."

Marianne Williamson says, "Joy is what happens when we allow ourselves to recognize how good things really are." So let's ask some questions here:

◊   *Are you looking to find your greatest joy?*
◊   *Do you even know what your greatest joy is?*
◊   *Do you really believe it is even possible?*
◊   *Even if you're happy (or not) right now, is there a simple way to feel even better?*

Ask yourself how you feel about your life right now? Are you getting all you need from it? Are you giving yourself all you need to feel happiness, or are you stuck in a job, a relationship, or a lifestyle that makes you unhappy. What can you do to change that?

Are you well on your way to accomplishing what you dreamed of doing, or are you still fumbling around trying to figure out what that looks like?

But then there is other side of the coin. What or who are you most proud of in your life. I'm most proud of my children. They have been subjected to some powerful challenges in their lifetime, and they are all taking responsibility for their part in it, and developing strong lives of their own. This is my greatest joy in life.

Another way to investigate how much joy there is in your life is to look at what kind of impact you made on other people. What are your accomplishments? Where have you taken risks and succeeded? All these are points of joy.

Finding joy in our life is not hard. It is the task of refocusing our attention away from the negative to the things that truly make the difference in our lives. Being grateful for the good things in life is where the joy lies. We are surrounded by opportunities to experience each and every day.

What Will it Take For You To Live Your Passion?

We are all a work in progress. We take each day as it comes and we explore and participate in what life has to offer. Getting from where you are now to where you want to be is a process of taking one step forward and perhaps, two steps back, but always with the intent to keep moving forward.

The fire gets extinguished when we keep a tight lid of the expectations, dreams and desires. Passion is life expressed in its fullness, and when we deny passion, we deny life. Fear is our passion dying to get out.

When we hold back and refuse to take the next step for fear of upsetting someone, of looking foolish, or being rejected, we are denying the life force. I did that for years. My most memorable metaphor was of standing in a large metal box with the lid on, the walls were all black and charred and I could smell the smoke. Up high on the far left corner of the box was a small door with light coming through it and I was trying to figure out how to get out of there. The box was a metaphor for the passion that was my fire, my light and my life. I am an extremely creative individual, but for years I didn't believe it. I told everyone I wasn't creative, even as I had learned how to live in foreign countries, had overcome all kinds of obstacles and I had written a soup cookbook. Creativity for me was not something I recognized, and yet I had dreamed about becoming a writer and a singer, both very creative acts. My passion was dying to get out, and I was afraid.

We make too many excuses for what we don't do and why we can't do it, and we frequently ask if it's okay for us to be doing something, instead of stepping up and saying, "This is what I need to do. This is what I will do. This is all about me, not you."

This is not selfish behavior. This is responsible behavior. It's the most positive, empowering thing you can do for yourself. It says loud and clear, I'm Important. You are important, and your needs should come first. They say you can't truly love another person until you learn to love yourself. I believe that to be true. I also know that until you start loving yourself, you will never be able to create passion in your life.

◊   So where in your life do you diminish your light?

◊   What do you do to limit your passion?

◊   Ask yourself what you care most deeply about and you will find your passion.

What Do You Need to (Start, Stop, Continue) Doing to Live Your Passion?

Living life with passion is what living the fulfilled life is all about.

In order for you to discover where your passion lies there are three steps you must take. The first is to identify your likes, dislikes and aptitudes. You did that in the skills and experience section of the book. You also identified your values, your beliefs and what drives your thoughts and behavior. And now you have an opportunity to complete a mission statement saying what it is you would like your life to be about.

Write it as if you were in it right now. Make sure that it is in the present tense and write it as if you were writing a story. Be specific and be visual. Engage all five senses when you write your mission statement. This is your life. Let your imagination go into overdrive as you bring your dreams into this statement. We will talk more about that later, but for now, let your passions drive your vision.

Describe what it looks like when you are doing the thing that you have identified as your passion. Remember what I said about permission. This is you giving yourself permission to build your life the way you want it. Once you've given yourself permission, you need to take action. Your passions are driven by a plan. Create a list of the positive outcomes you will experience as a result of living your passions. Who will benefit and what are the expected rewards. Then figure out what it will take to make this happen. What resources will you need to move forward? Is it time, money, people, things? Who is going to help you get where you want to go. This is critical because we can't do these changes alone. I had a whole army of people behind me willing me to succeed, supporting me and helping me grow my confidence. Be specific about what you need to develop your passion. If you need to develop new skills, what does that look like? If you need to change jobs, what does that look like? Then take the action steps necessary to make it happen. A dream without a goal is just a fantasy. Make it real by making it concrete. That means making it visible to yourself in whatever way you can. Make a vision board, collecting photos or articles that are a part of what you feel passionate about. Write action lists, and set deadlines to reach your goals. All of these steps are critical to making it real for you.

Let your passion evolve. Share your enthusiasm for your subject with others. Invite others into your dream. Give yourself the opportunity to do things differently and see how it feels. I used to say to my kids when they said they didn't want something, even before they had tried, "you have to try it once. If you don't like it, then fine. I'm not going to force you to do something you don't want." That's how we learn what works.

Tales from the Trail
"Finding My Way"—Bethany Brown

I was one year out of college with a degree in English and Mass Media Communications, full of enthusiasm for the future, and at a total loss as to what I wanted to do with my life. Instead of rushing off to a high paying, professional career, I spent my first year as a college graduate waiting tables at a local restaurant and living with my parents—not at all what I had expected when I walked across the stage and accepted my diploma!

Whether it was fear or comfort that kept me from leaving the nest, I still don't know, and in truth, it was probably a little of both. What I did know for sure was I was stuck and I couldn't continue down the path I was on. It was time for me to make a drastic change to break the small town cycle that has engulfed so many in my graduating class—past, present and future.

On a rainy Ohio afternoon, I printed out and mailed over fifty resumes to companies throughout the United States. At the time, I don't recall having a good understanding about what I could actually do with my hard earned degree. I just knew that I wanted to do *something*, and I didn't care what 'it' would be. I would send my hopes out into the universe and wait for recruiters and HR managers to come clamoring for my services.

The question was, where would I go and what would I do? And could I get over my fear of leaving home? I had already done it once going to college, but somehow it seemed different this time. I was going into the "real world" of jobs, getting my own apartment, paying bills and taking care of myself without support. This would be the biggest risk of my life.

As fate would have it, two very different job opportunities presented themselves within days of each other. One required that I drive just 45 minutes to interview for a management position at a local restaurant. Since the restaurant was part of an established chain, this job paid very well and offered two weeks of vacation per year. Also, it was located just a short distance from home in an area with a very low cost of living. Many recent college graduates would consider it a dream come true, but I knew if I did this, I would regret it for the rest of my life.

The other required that I travel to Boston for an interview with a small book publisher. This was more like it. But it came with a price. As they were on a tight budget, they did not pay my expenses to go interview with them. So I collected my tips, booked my own airfare, and paid close to $100 in cab fare (each way) to take a copyediting and proofreading test for an entry-level job. For those that don't know the book business, entry level jobs pay next to nothing, and it was based in the second-most-expensive city in the United States. It would also take me far from friends and family and would require me to room with strangers, as well as learn a new city and industry on my own.

My parents wanted me to take the restaurant job. It was safe. There was security. It paid well. It would keep me close to home. Part of me agreed wholeheartedly. It was safe and secure, and it did pay well...but it wasn't enough. The job in Boston offered none of these comforts, but it did give me something more: it was a chance to work in the publishing world. Every English majors dream!

I went back and forth until I realized it was a make or break situation. If I stayed, I would forever feel like I could have done more, and if I went, it would be scary to be alone, having to adjust to a new situation, but like going to college I reasoned, I would eventually get used to it.

Two weeks later, with a van packed full of all of my worldly goods, I began the cross-country drive to my new life in New York City. I found roommates online, signed a lease via fax, and resigned myself to cheap beer, cigarettes and canned food for the next several months. The job offered no guarantees, no safety net, and no real promise for a future. In fact, it would take more than half of my monthly salary just to pay my third of the rent. I was terrified. But I decided the fear was worth facing, and I showed up for work.

Now more than ten years later, I look back on that decision as the best I've ever made. I could have stayed home, worked in the restaurant business and bought a house just a short drive from my family. I could have let the instant security keep me in my safe little box in Northeastern Ohio.

Instead, I ventured out and began a career that has led me to managing multi-million dollar book series, launching major new imprints and ultimately working in my favorite industry on my own terms as a consultant.

I'd like to say it was easy. I'd like to say that every decision I've made since then has been made confidently and fearlessly. But that would be a lie.

Each time fear strikes, I can look back at my 22 year-old self and remember, sometimes the decisions you make in the face of fear are those than can change your life drastically for the better.

Stepping into the Jungle

Ask Yourself:

What does PASSION mean to you?

What is your favorite thing to do? Why?

Where in your life do you experience the most joy? Why?

What are you willing to stop/start/continue doing to live your passion?

Where in life do you seek permission to do what pleases you?

What would you like to achieve? Why is that important to you?

What are you doing to reach your goals? When will you start to see results?

CHAPTER 15
Respect Your Intentions

ᴬᴬᴬ

"Instead of looking at life as a narrowing funnel, we can see it ever-widening to choose the things we want to do, to take the wisdoms we've learned and create something."—Liz Carpenter

Go Ahead. It's YOUR turn.

Where in Life Do You Take Risks?

One day, I was standing waiting on the NYC subway to go downtown, staring at the tiles on the wall thinking about how grubby they were, when my eyes settled on one word written vertically—RISK. It got me thinking about how many risks we take on a daily basis. We take risks just crossing the street, getting in our car, going into the subway, flying on an airplane. These are ordinary risks we take for granted. But the word risk came to me in a different form. I saw it as Respect your Intention and Show Kourage.

Risk that what you want is attainable; risk that you won't lose your relationship as a result of following your dreams; risk

239

that you won't lose your job because you speak up about the dissatisfaction you may be feeling; risk that you may fail at achieving your desires. When you give yourself permission to create the life you want, you take a risk. When you respect your intentions and show kourage, you take action. That's the next logical step.

Every decision we make carries with it some degree of risk. It is almost impossible for us to have any degree of satisfaction in life without taking risks. All our joy, success and adventure in life is discovered by taking risks. You have discovered that when applying for a new job, deciding where to live, who to marry, or not, what things you like to do, the pleasures you experience in life. You took a risk when you decided to open up this book to see what was in it. Hopefully, there are enough good ideas to change your life. This is a massive risk. We risk our lives when we cross the street. I live in NYC and you better have your head on straight when you're in midtown. I was once run-over by a car because I didn't look both ways crossing the street. I presumed it was a one-way. That was a huge risk I took in that presumption. It didn't pay off. All risks are the result of our courage, knowledge and beliefs. We choose to play it safe, or we choose to take risks. When we risk, we learn more, we experience more, and we open ourselves to opportunities we may not have had if we played it safe. There are a million examples of what that looks like and I'll leave it to you to figure out where you are playing safe or are taking risks.

Sam Keen, the author of Fire in the Belly said, "fear is the sharp edge of excitement." When I heard that in one of his workshops, I felt that sharp edge running up my spine. I have spent the better part of my life on that sharp edge, and often referred to myself as living on the edge because I had been taking huge risks since I was young. I stole from my parents and others, did drugs, left home with no money and no place to stay, had unprotected sex with many different partners, and moved to another country without knowing anyone and no money. At the time, I didn't think risk I thought survival. But these were the risks I took, and more. My life has been a series of risks, no doubt yours has been too.

Risk is the chance that something may go wrong. There is no certainty in life. If you were a mountain climber on Mt. Everest and were unprepared, you would be risking your life. Gamblers risk their fortune. Drug users risk their lives. Most of us don't go looking for dramatic adventures. We're quite happy dealing with the ones that are close to home.

Here are just a few of the ways in which you can take risks:
- ◊ Say NO more often.
- ◊ Talk with Significant Others about what is important to you.
- ◊ Learn something new.
- ◊ Honor your feelings.
- ◊ Set boundaries with the people in your life.
- ◊ Take care of your body and mind.
- ◊ Give up some of the control and delegate.
- ◊ Have more fun.
- ◊ Laugh more often.

Expressing your physical self carelessly, making silly jokes or silly observations, is liberating. It drives my daughters mad when I behave in a silly fashion. Of course, they don't call it silly, they just think it's plain old stupid and embarrassing, even if no one else is in the room. I have learned to love having fun, making fun, and laughing like crazy. I have been known to say something really stupid at the table, and to find my own jokes so hilarious that I laugh until I cry. Then I get everyone else around the table to laugh hysterically too as they watch me having a meltdown.

One morning, I woke my then eleven-year-old daughter for school. She was having a hard time with a particular school in Paris because she felt totally out of place, and I knew she did not want to get up because it was physical fitness day. She told me that the idea of physical fitness at the school was to play ping-pong, also known as table tennis, or badminton, and since coordination is not her strong suit, she was reluctant to make a fool of herself. So I crawled into bed with her and told her the story of Ping and Pong, the Chinese acrobats. I was so caught up in the ridiculousness of Ping and Pong that we both started to laugh hysterically until the tears were running down our faces.

I have created many moments like this in my children's lives. It is good for me. Laugh until you cry. It's a cleansing of the soul. Learn how to play again.

Where in Life Do You Avoid Risk?

Most of the risks we take in life won't kill us, but they can certainly put us under tremendous emotional strain. We avoid things that bring us pain. It's human nature. If I take a risk by changing my career, I'm putting my family in jeopardy financially. I may not have enough to support them. If I decide that it's more important for me to be single after thirty years of marriage, I'm taking a huge risk that I'll be okay living on my own. And it can also be something very simple. I'm going to wash the car today even if it looks like it might rain.

Risks are a part of life. We all take them big and small, and how you choose to manage them is what makes the difference. We avoid risks when we don't have enough information, or when we think we will suffer as a result of taking one. But many of the risks you avoid today will come back to haunt you. By committing yourself to the change process, to developing a life filled with passion and fulfillment, you are taking risks. Growing and changing is risky business, but there is one thing we all know. The only constant in life is change, and we must risk all to truly meet the demands it places upon us. Taking a risk is not about what other people feel, do or think. It's about what it does for you. How does it improve the quality of your life?"

RISK

The ultimate goal of risk is to learn and grow as a result of the experiences we've had. When we set our intention towards a goal, and we show courage to meet whatever demands it places upon us, then we are living life authentically. When we are living intentionally, we are taking action and taking full responsibility for the outcome. This takes courage. The idea of living our lives conditioned by choices and decisions is a courageous one. We move forward with intention towards our goals. We set our intention for success. Our intention for health. Our intention for a life well-lived. Showing up to life in all its colors and textures is the risk we take. Sometimes it works, and sometimes it doesn't. We are failing our way towards success. We are taking the risks necessary to create the life we want. We are creating our best life now.

What does that look like?

You won't know until you take the risk to find out.

Tales from the Trail
"The Door Slammed, Now What?"—Annie Teich

Even if your boss cries when he lets you go, you are still fired. What do you do when you find yourself at mid-life losing the best job you've ever had—a job that is the best fit for your talents and gifts, and paying the most money you've ever made? There is nothing that can prevent the feeling of rejection when you realize your services are no longer required and you no longer have a professional home or a safety net.

I give full credit to my sister for asking a fateful question as I cried in my sink: "Don't you think it's about time you took all the passion you've given to building other people's companies and build your own?"

With the proverbial slap to the forehead, I responded slowly, "Yes, I could do that." Suddenly the opportunity to be my own boss presented itself, and even though I had never seriously considered it, the moment to decide that very thing had arrived.

Once the idea began percolating in my brain, my raging pity party came to an end, and I immediately began making plans. As soon as I started saying such things out loud as, "I wonder if that vendor would sell those titles to me," I was off and running. After all, I had worked in the educational publishing business for more than twenty years. I had helped a number of companies grow their product lines and their businesses. Certainly I could do that for myself? I had spent most of my career working for entrepreneurs and believed I had a sufficient understanding of the personal commitment required, plus I was confident I had the energy, determination, and drive to launch and grow a successful company.

After living in an historic home for more than nineteen years, my husband and I purchased a new home—and moved in exactly three weeks before I was fired from my *perfect* job. In the process, of course, we had significantly increased our mortgage. What initially seemed like a calamity, turned out to be a blessing. I did not realize it at the time, but the house and its equity line were bankable assets that allowed me to launch, not one, but two businesses simultaneously. It was only the first of a series of providential opportunities that came my way over the next two years.

It is true that, had I known how difficult this journey would be, I would probably have done the normal thing and just looked for another job. But because my children are grown and gone, and because I'm an optimistic *can-do* person by nature, in the end I chose this path because I didn't want to get to the end of my life saying, "I coulda, woulda, shoulda." Even in the face of total failure, the worst outcome I saw was selling the house and getting a new job. Since we'd already moved away from the home where we raised our children, having to sell this new house didn't seem awful, and I would still be employable.

Acknowledging that you can live with the worst-case scenario doesn't make the fear of failure disappear. I'm not sure it ever does. But there is great value in determining the worst of the possibilities before you. If you decide that you can handle the direst outcome, then there is absolutely no reason why you shouldn't jump into an adventure and countless reasons why you should.

So without any preparation of any kind, I made the leap. Almost immediately, I began to receive the benefit of a strong professional network and the heartfelt support of industry colleagues and friends. People don't do business with companies. They do business with people they like. And when you are in an industry like K–12 publishing and hit a speed bump, you quickly find out who your friends and supporters are. Friends and acquaintances literally came out of the woodwork to cheer me on and actively sought opportunities to provide me consulting work to pay the bills while I worked at launching the company.

I have begun calling myself a *simultaneous* entrepreneur instead of the more common *serial* entrepreneur. It is probably true that if I had launched one business instead of two, I would be twice as far ahead as I currently am. However, the learning opportunities have been manifold and exciting. And the most amazing thing has been that every single obstacle has been overcome—in some instances from unexpected or surprising sources.

So here is a synopsis of what I have learned in the last twenty-one months.

- ◊   We are stronger than we think we are.
- ◊   People are kinder than we think they are.
- ◊   You don't have to imagine your future in detail to create it.
- ◊   Getting up every day to work hard at moving forward creates its own momentum.
- ◊   Friends keep you honest.

◊   If you think you understand how much work is involved, triple it.

◊   Being able to laugh in general, and at yourself in particular, is good medicine.

◊   Backing up to go forward is often a wise thing.

◊   And finally, waiting until you're ready to launch your business is like waiting to have children. If you wait until the optimal moment, it might never happen. So, be brave. Seize the opportunity when it presents itself. Reinvent yourself in your fifties. All the best people are doing it.

"Don't live down to expectations. Go out there and do something remarkable."—Wendy Wasserstein.

Stepping into the Jungle

Ask Yourself:

Where in your life do you take risks? Are they physical, emotional or spiritual?

Where do you avoid risks? What is that about for you?

Where do you take risks in relationships? Are they risks that cause you harm?

Are you playing it 'safe' in life by staying in your 'comfort' zone?

How often are you willing to say NO when something doesn't work for you?

What are you doing to learn something new each day?

What are you willing to give up control off so you can meet your goals?

What would a risky life look like to you?

Notes

PART 4
MASTER THE JUNGLE

Notes

CHAPTER 16
Play a Bigger Game

✿✿✿

"Most people never run far enough on their first wind to find out they've got a second. Give your dreams all you've got and you'll be amazed at the energy that comes from you."—William James

Life demands that we play big. It doesn't shrink from giving us all it's got, so why should we give it any less.

What Does It Mean to Play a Bigger Game?

Each of us is born with extraordinary potential, and we all possess the unique ability to create positive change in our lives. Playing a bigger game means you are hungry for something more. You are searching for fulfillment, and you are searching for meaning and purpose in your life. You want to share the fruits of your knowledge and experience with others and make a difference in the world. That's playing a bigger game.

When I undertook the business of motivating people to go beyond their fears, doubts and anxieties, I could have created a career as a life-coach, and settled for that, but I knew there was something more I wanted to do. I wanted to write about it, speak about it, and deliver my message to millions of people because I felt it was important enough to get out there. That was my bigger game.

Being in your greatness doesn't mean you are better than others. It simply means you are living authentically. You are living from the core of your being, stripped of all the false beliefs, facades, and limitations you have placed on yourself. It is the place of power that exists within all of us. It is also a scary place because there is nowhere to hide. But then again, why would you want to? There is nothing to hide. You are a magnificent being in mind, body, and spirit, and the only person who can make you less than that is YOU.

It took me a long time to realize I was constantly giving my power away to other people. I made them greater than me. I made them more talented, more beautiful, more caring, more, more, more. When you invest your power in other people they will willingly take it. Who doesn't want to be flattered by others? People are such insecure creatures that any attention is good attention, right? Wrong. We frequently invest our greatness in the wrong people because of insecurity. Stepping away from that is a huge challenge, but it can be done if there is a will to do so.

Starting Fearless Fifties was one of the most amazing leaps of faith I have ever undertaken. I felt like a complete fake. I had no business background, limited experience as a speaker and workshop leader, and was relatively new to working with people one-on-one in the coaching business. But I did have something very important—a burning desire to teach what I had learned over a lifetime of stepping off the cliff.

Many people get caught up in life, feeling like they're just waiting to get caught. It's a 'fake it till you make it', but even after you've 'made' it, you still feel like someone will catch you out. So many women—highly successful women—feel this way. I felt that way for the longest time. If I *looked* credible, then people would believe I was competent. But inside, I wasn't sure. I looked really great on the surface but inside I was still playing SMALL.

I didn't believe I was coming from my authentic source. I was more than competent, I was really good at what I did, and in any moment of clarity, I could feel it; but there was a nagging place...the fear that I really couldn't compete with the professionals I met regularly, or who had more experience than me. Of course, I knew they had once been where I am, and for all I knew, were still there.

I cried when I heard this Mariannne Williamson quote:

"Our deepest fear is not that we are inadequate. Our deepest fear is that we are powerful beyond measure. It is our light, not our darkness that most frightens us. We ask ourselves, Who am I to be brilliant, gorgeous, talented, fabulous? Actually, who are you not to be? You are a child of God. Your playing small does not serve the world. There is nothing enlightened about shrinking so that other people won't feel insecure around you. We are all meant to shine, as children do. We were born to make manifest the glory of God that is within us. It's not just in some of us; it's in everyone. And as we let our own light shine, we unconsciously give other people permission to do the same. As we are liberated from our own fear, our presence automatically liberates others. "—Marianne Williamson

It was clear that I was playing small in order to protect myself from the imagined ridicule, rejection, or dismissal that would come from stepping right up to the plate and saying, "Yes, I know what I'm doing. Yes, I'm pretty good at this. Yes, I have much to learn, and will continue to learn until the day I die." But more importantly, in playing LARGE, I'm giving the world my gift. It took me three occasions in front of my teachers to finally get this part of the puzzle. I stood in a room of two-hun-dred-fifty people and admitted I had been playing small and cried. I gave myself permission to let go of that place. I am not small, have never been small except, as I have allowed myself to be. I spent my life seeking approval from others. It has been a major impediment to being LARGE. I needed permission. I have fought it most of my life, but as one wise teacher told me, "You will truly come into your own when you can reach a place where the approval of others is no longer necessary." I'm still working on that part.

You play a bigger game when you choose to be surrounded by people who are already playing at the top of their game, or you are creating something that is beyond your limited and local presence. You play a bigger game when you are willing to risk all to make a difference in the world. It's about what happens when you take risks and you start living your purpose.

What Do You Think is Holding You Back?

You cannot move into your greatness without confronting your fears. You must confront the things that scare you the most if you are to grow to your full height and become the woman you were meant to be. We are all born with a Divine Presence. We are all part of that force which unites us in nature. We are all in relationship to everyone and everything. For each cause there is an effect. For every action there is a reaction. It is the Laws of Nature and the Law of the Universe from which we all come, and to which we are all related. When you deny your life force, you deny Nature, and when you deny Nature, you have stopped growing, because everything in nature is organic. If you're not growing, you're dying. When you refuse the call of Nature, the call of YOU to show up to YOU, then you are stifling your growth.

Despair is born out of a refusal to move beyond the limitations of where you are. Everyone has the right to choose his or her existence.

Everyone has a right to reject limiting behavior from others and especially from themselves.

Everyone has the right to create and live the kind of life they want to live.

Circumstances are only roadblocks. You can remove them if you have the courage to break loose. When you are stepping into your greatness, you are removing the blinds from your eyes and the earplugs from your ears; you are taking the rag out of your mouth and standing on your own two feet embracing everything that comes your way, both good and bad. EVERYTHING is an opportunity for growth. Everything is an opportunity to explore how GREAT you can be.

> *"How easy to be amiable in the midst of happiness*
> *and success."*—Anne Sophie Swetchine

Who is moved to tears by a person who stands up and says, "I have had a very easy life and I am pretty happy today?" You want to hear the person who says, "Life was tough, it got harder, then there was some suffering. I should have given up, there was no way to survive it all, but I held on for one more minute until I was able to emerge triumphant, and here I am."

I recently heard the remarkable story of Immaculee Illibagiza, author of *Left To Tell,* who told how she hid in a bathroom in Rwanda for ninety days while, outside, her entire family and village were butchered by Hutus. That is a story to make you celebrate your own life. And make you celebrate the indomitable human spirit.

We play small because we think we are safer staying in the shadows, not making a noise, not wanting to be seen. Many people don't want the attention on them because they don't feel adequate to the task. They worry that people will find out they are faking it. Not really up to the task at hand. Other excuses are not having enough resources. Not enough money. Not enough time. Not enough connection. Not enough ME. There are a multitude of reasons that hold people back from playing in a bigger arena, but none of them are valid.

We hold ourselves small because we are afraid we are not big enough.

We think that by entering a bigger playing field life will become more stressful, busier and more difficult. Well, the answer is, it probably will. I'm busier than I've ever been, but I'm also feeling more fulfilled. It's certainly more stressful living this kind of life, and I'm challenged on a daily basis with decisions I have learned how to make, and choices that will affect the future. But I keep on doing it because I believe I'm doing something worthwhile. I believe my purpose in life is to be doing exactly what it is I'm doing. It's my passion.

But interestingly, the more engaged I am in the work I'm doing, the less stressful life seems to be. This is the paradox. I have way more going on in my life on a daily basis than I ever did before, and I feel more engaged in life than ever before.

I trained in martial arts for fifteen years and I discovered that the secret to success is simple.

◊ Commitment

◊ Focus

◊ Determination

◊ Courage

◊ Follow-Through.

With these elements in place the outcome is assured. There is no resistance to change. In a fight, you must have all these elements in place if you are to win. But it's not about violence. It's simply about methodology. These are the elements that add up to any successful endeavor.

History is replete with people who played a bigger game and changed the course of history.

◊ H.H. The Dalai Lama

◊ Bill Gates

◊ Jonas Salk

◊ Martin Luther King

◊ Rosa Parks

◊   Mother Theresa

◊   Richard Branson

◊   Barak Obama

The one thing that differentiates these people from us ordinary mortals is they had a vision. They believed in something that was much greater than they were. They played for much higher stakes that would influence the world. That's playing a HUGE game. But for the rest of us mortals, our playing a bigger game is simply learning how to be in the world in a bigger way. Making a difference in our lives and in the lives of others.

Who Do You Need To Be To Play In a Bigger Game?

So where in your life are you playing small? What do you need to do to expand your vision? Is it simply putting a game plan in place? Is it about thinking bigger? What can you do to take more risks and allow yourself to experience the uncertainty of outcome? Are you holding yourself back by telling yourself you're not capable, you're not good enough, you're not rich enough, you're not enough?

What would it take for you to feel like you're playing for higher stakes? How much do you need to adjust your vision, get support, create a different plan than the one you've got going on at this moment?

Who do you need to be to play a bigger game?

I needed to be more confident that I had all the skills necessary to be in the game? I had to feel supported by the people around me, and receive feedback about where I was playing small. I needed to know how it was not serving me, and more importantly, it was not serving the people I wanted to connect with in the world. When you play a bigger game, you have a responsibility to yourself and to the world to deliver what you promise. This responsibility to be who you are comes with a price tag. You must be willing to take the risks otherwise you're not playing a bigger game, you're simply watching the action.

Answer the following questions:

◊ Do you long for something new?

◊ Are you longing for a more meaningful and fulfilling life?

◊ Do you want to make a difference in the world and you're not sure what that looks like?

◊ Are you ready for a change, but you don't know how?

◊ Are you ready to take risks?

◊ If you answered yes to any of these questions, you are ready to play a bigger game so ask yourself:

◊ Who do I need to be?

◊ What do I want to get?

◊ What will it take for me to get there?

◊ What can I expect to achieve when I play the bigger game?

What Do You Need to Do To Start/Stop/Continue Doing to Play A Bigger Game?

Look around your life and see where you limit how you express yourself.

◊ What behaviors are currently getting in your way?

◊ How do you hold back from speaking your truth?

◊ What excites you but you tone it down because you don't want to offend anyone, or you don't want to appear too arrogant, big or aggressive?

◊ What is out there that pulls you in, and creates a juicy feeling of excitement when you're engaged in it?

◊ What people in your life inspire you to stretch further, and who can you enlist to help you reach your goals?

◊ What are you willing to give up to play in a bigger arena?

◊ Where in your life do you sacrifice and under serve your vision?

◊ Where is your passion leading you?

Answer these questions and you will have a greater idea of how you can play in a bigger arena and reach your goals.

Tales from the Trail
"The Lioness Mother"—Die Fietjes

Throughout my life I have struggled against a constant feeling of *not enough*. My mother believes it began before I was born. She was pregnant with me in Borneo, now known as Kalimantan, after the Second World War, during the war of Independence in Indonesia. My father, who had been interned in Japanese war camps, was sent to Borneo to keep the peace amongst the Dajaks, who were headhunters. She spoke many times of the difficulties they faced at that time, and how there was always a need for something to make life comfortable. She says that my feeling of never having enough may have come from this experience.

Most of my life she tried to limit my wants. If I asked for things, she would tell me it wasn't good to ask for things, or she would tell me she was disappointed I had asked. That gave me the feeling it wasn't right to express my needs or my wants, and I felt guilty even for *thinking* of things I wanted. I felt guilty before I even asked! Now, at age sixty-one, I am still uncomfortable sharing my desires.

Through Cranio-Sacral Therapy, I had the experience of going back to the time I was no bigger than a kidney glued to wall of my mother's womb, listening hard to what was going on outside; I felt anxious, insecure, preparing myself for what was coming. This experience instilled the idea that life is ruled by fear and I was using all my energy to prepare for the attack. My way of thinking about how to survive that attack has kept my panic under control, but just barely.

So here I am writing about being Fear*less*. How do you get from there to here? The moments when I overcame fear were always times when I was too busy surviving to indulge in anxiety—like the time I went to Portugal with my sons, who were twenty-one and nineteen at the time. We swam and played in the clear cold water, resting and sharing a picnic on the rocks. And then some kids, boys and girls alike, climbed the highest rock, at least nine meters high, and jumped down into the water. I watched and enjoyed their fearless flying leaps. I would never dare such a thing, not with my extreme fear of heights. Still, something urged me to climb to that point and look. The view was incredible, looking down was scary. The kids who jumped were elated. Something inside me wanted to join in that emotion. They urged me on: "You can do it."

The friend who took us there had been down in the water to make sure the kids were safe, and one of them urged me to take the plunge, saying that he would see me through the leap. Somehow, in a split second, I decided to let go of my fear and jump. I soared through the air for seconds—for eternity in the here and now—and then splashed into the water. I jumped with fear and then lost it on the way down. I was elated and felt ever so happy. I did it. My sons and their young friends were very happy for me too.

When my first son Daniel was born, I was nearly twenty-eight. The pregnancy was not without fears, but the birth was perfect, pain and all. In those days (and, to a certain extent, still now) I was very much inclined to be perfect—a perfect wife and lover, a perfect housewife, a perfect mother. I was fiercely protective of my relationship, and strongly afraid I would not be good enough. Our son was one-month-old and my husband, an artist, was given an assignment in London to do a mural. During that time he met a woman, and after much hesitation, I left my home in Amsterdam to go rescue my marriage in London. I was not fearless because I found it very difficult to speak up for myself, but the mother in me made it possible. We reconciled, but two years later our marriage crumbled again when he fell in love with a woman who came to clean for us.

I was in the midst of planning a trip to Goa and Indonesia with our sons, aged two and five. And just before we left, I had a miscarriage—which at the time was better than the abortion I had planned. I was all over the place emotionally, didn't have much money, and I got caught shoplifting in Boots, the chemist. So I left for the trip with a court case hanging over me for the next four months. After our trip, we arrived home to find that my husband was still in the affair, and had used our home and our cottage in Cornwall with her while we were gone.

When we finally divorced in 1982, he left with the words, "You wanted to have children, you can have them." At that point, my world finally collapsed. I had done my utmost to keep the family together, but the ground under my feet disappeared, I had to bundle all my strength to live with my fear, to overcome it for the sake of my children.

Although my children never had the pleasure of having a father, when his wife died in 2008, our youngest son offered his father support. I knew it was hard, but I was proud of him for doing this. Our oldest son has not been able to take that step yet. I was brave enough and fearless enough to raise them by myself, and I will support them no matter what happens.

That is something a mother will do, no matter what. She is the fearless lioness for her cubs—always.

"If we keep on doin' what we always done, we'll keep on gettin' what we always got."—Barbara Lyons

Stepping into the Jungle

Ask Yourself:

Do you feel like you're living up to your potential? If not, what would it take for you to feel that way?

Are you living authentically, being true to who you are as defined by you? If not, what barriers do you need to remove in order to play in a bigger arena?

Are you making conscious choices which lead you upwards towards your goals? If not, what would it take to make that happen?

Do you seek other people's approval before you step up to what you want? If so, then what would it look like if you were to let that go?

Are you surrounded by people who are playing a bigger game? Who do you need to be to bring them into your circle?

Are you ready to be an inspiration to others who look to you as a model for the change process? If so, what will it take for you to get there?

What do you need to start/stop/continue doing to play a bigger game?

"Life has to be lived, that's all there is to it."—Eleanor Roosevelt

CHAPTER 17
Take Control

"To get up each morning with the resolve to be happy... is to set our own conditions to the events of each day. To do this is to condition circumstances instead of being conditioned by them."—Ralph Waldo Emerson

Living in fear is the direct result of not trusting you have control of the car you are driving.

Choose the life YOU want. It is Yours. You Own it. No one else does.

Where In Your Life Do You Give Up Control?

This is an interesting question. We all have areas of our life where we allow others to control us because we don't speak up, we don't take action, we don't participate freely, or we resist through passive aggressive behavior.

You allow others to control your life when you don't speak up for what you believe. When you hold back on your opinions for fear you'll be seen as ridiculous, or unimportant. When you allow others to make decisions for you, you are relinquishing control. In short, you are not taking responsibility for yourself.

When you are spending your life trying to please others, they are essentially controlling you. You may not even realize it's happening. You're just aware that there is little time for what you want, and it becomes a problem. You don't feel like you're living your own life.

If you are experiencing any of the following then you are not in control of your life:

◊   Someone in your life is very needy and you feel you must save him or her.

◊   They tell you that you don't love them if you don't do something for them

◊   Tell you how much they've done for you, and therefore imply that it's your turn

◊   Suffer from many petty illnesses that draw your attention away from your needs

◊   Don't honor you requests to do something for you because they're too busy

◊   You give up your own plans regularly because it would make someone feel better

◊   You rarely make your own decision without consulting someone first

These are all symptoms of allowing others to control you and in order to live life on your own terms, you have to understand that you can't please everyone all the time, and the only person you can change is YOU. That means that trying to control the behavior of others is a waste of time. Allowing people to have their own ways, even when they don't work for you, takes courage. When in conflict, you can choose to engage or not. You can decide if this is really about the other person, or examine your reactions and see if it's your stuff that's getting in the way. But this takes confidence.

You already know you can't make changes without taking action. You have to learn how to face the things in your life that make you want to recoil, where you are afraid it will compromise the status quo or so-called 'comfort' zone, where some of your deepest anxieties reside. Taking action is incredibly empowering. You feel good when you feel you are taking control of your life.

So why don't people do it more often?

Because they're stuck. Stuck in jobs, relationships, routines, bad health. People stick to what they know, stick to the familiar, stick to the old routines. The glue that keeps them in place is suffocating them, however.

Do you know these terrible glue strips that get put down to catch mice? The mouse wrestles with being stuck, but ultimately can't set itself free and expires from the effort it took trying to be free. The mouse didn't have a choice. It was stuck good and proper for a good reason—to die there. You, on the other hand, have a choice. You can exercise your free will.

But you may often get stuck, and it doesn't feel good. You suffer the discomfort, the uncertainty, the frustration and resentment because you're not taking action to move forward. Have you heard the phrase, *Better the devil you know than the one you don't know?* Well, who needs to keep company with a medieval ideology anyway? Why do you have to have a devil in your life at all? Isn't the devil just the glue that keeps people stuck in negative thinking, limiting behaviors, and a blocked view of the world that could be? I don't need to have that imagery in my life, thank you very much, and neither do you.

There is a proverb that says, "A man must do. A woman need only be." As a woman, I think that's rather passive. Remember, I'm the human do-er and I'm a woman! But there's something else in that. When you learn how to be, you allow yourself to discover the meaning of who you are and what your purpose is in life. Making meaning out of the things you do in life is the main reason you exist happily or otherwise. Getting clarity is a life mission.

So what have you learned in life? Where are your actions taking you? What plans are you making, what dreams do you want to see realized, what changes do you want to make to move yourself out of the stuck places? Make a list of all the areas in your life you want to change—your body, your work, your relationships, your health, your money, whatever—and then make a list of all the ways in which you can reach the goals you set for yourself.

There is an expression that "you can't teach an old dog new tricks", but I believe you can certainly teach an old *broad* new tricks. You are never too old to change, to learn new things. I hope I continue learning until the day I die, because there is so much to be learned in life. When you stop, you die. Take life by the reigns and guide it, otherwise you're the one being whipped into shape.

Do You 'Think' You Can?

"If you think you can, you can. And if you think you can't, you're right."—Henry Ford.

Confidence comes from believing in you. You already know this. But for many of us, it doesn't come naturally. I had the self-esteem of a gnat for years. Developing confidence in your abilities demands that you put some serious effort into changing the messages in your head. We've covered a lot of that in the book so I'm not going to belabor it here again. But it comes down to this at all levels when we're making personal changes.

The choices you make each day, big and small, build your life. If you are walking around as the victim of bad luck, vindictive neighbors, or a rotten family—get over it. You choose, *each day*, to be in a job you don't like, to stay friends with a toxic person, to try and make a cold person love you, and this only succeeds in guaranteeing you misery.

The question to ask yourself is this: Are you a victim? Or, does your actions indicate you are taking responsibility for your own life?

Be careful with this one, because many claim they are taking responsibility even though they are quick to blame, to judge, and to negate the other people in their lives. A person who is living life to the fullest doesn't have any interest in engaging in destructive activities. What is the point?

Realize your own self-destructive behavior, but don't waste time punishing yourself over it. The moment you recognize this pattern, something wonderful happens. You can release it and begin to make healthy choices, take actions that assertively build the life you deserve. Step to the side, get out of your own way, and watch the magic begin before your eyes. This is not to imply that the whole world will toss rose petals at you when you walk down the sidewalk. There will be unpleasantness and trials ahead. But you do not have to fall down wailing and thrashing about—unless you really want to.

Be in choice, not in doubt. Be in celebration, not in guilt or worry.

Be in Life, not in stagnation. These are your choices.

Make the decision today to live your best life now. There is no tomorrow because it's not here yet. There is only this moment now. That's the only true reality. The rest is mind games. You have a choice. Use it wisely.

Remember the story of The Little Engine That Could? As it climbed the hill, it wasn't sure if it had enough steam to make it up and over to save the village on the other side. But it kept saying, "I think I can, I think I can, I think I can," until it reached the crest of the hill and was able to cruise down on the other side. That's the image I get when I think of building confidence. Lack of confidence holds you back from achieving the life you want. It stops you from becoming the person you want to be. It creeps into everything. Your relationships, your work, your expectations and desires, and it kills the dream. You're reading this because you want the dream. You want to play in a bigger game and you want to know how it's done.

Confident people believe in themselves and they succeed because of it.

So how confident are you?

Rate the following statements from 0-10 based on how much you believe each of them to be true.

0 would mean you don't believe in the statement at all
10 would mean you think it's completely true.

I like myself as a person   _____
I am as good as everyone else   _____
When I look in the mirror I like what I see   _____
I don't feel like an overall failure   _____
I am happy to be me   _____
I respect myself   _____
I'd rather be me than anyone else   _____
What others say to me has no affect   _____
I enjoy communicating with others   _____
I have the skills to make life a success   _____
I like to take risks   _____
I am not afraid to make mistakes   _____
I can laugh at myself   _____
Now sum up your scores: _____

If you have scored:
100-130 You have a high level of self-esteem and confidence. All you have to do is fine tune it and increase your confidence in a couple of areas.

65-99 You have a medium to high ranking in self-esteem. While most of the time you are okay, there are times when you can feel rock bottom. You need more consistency that you are confident and learn to experience that more regularly.

3-64 You have low levels of self-esteem. You lack confidence in yourself in most areas and need to have an overall confidence-building plan.

0-29 You have reached rock bottom and think that everyone is against you. You are stuck in a rut and need to get out of it quick.

Write down some of the observations you made while taking this assessment. What do you specifically need to concentrate on to build up your confidence? I'll bet that it's not in all areas that you need to do some changing. It's probably only in a few. Try taking the Life Evaluator at the end of the book and see how you add up on the score chart.

Developing confidence is a daily practice.

To learn more about building your confidence check out the bonus offer at the end of the book.

No More Distractions

I love to be distracted! As I'm writing this section my Twitter Twhirl floats into view and I can't resist going to see who was replying to me. (My coach Stephanie Frank), and I'm aware that as an ADD adult, it's all too easy for me to shift my attention over there instead of staying on task. Do you have that same problem? Maybe not because you're an ADD person, but because it's a human thing; we all love to be distracted, particularly if it's something you don't want to be doing, (which is not the case here. I love to write.)

Learning how to stay focused takes discipline and a commitment to the outcome. In my case, I want to get this draft of the manuscript finished in the next day or so, so I must stay on task to complete my goal.

Distracted in the dictionary means mentally confused, troubled or remote. If this is how you run your day, then it's time to get clear. I also like to align distraction with procrastination. I can find all kinds of reasons why I'm not doing something because I've got a list a mile long elsewhere to attend to. I forget things, or misplace them because my mind is on something else, so staying focused takes a lot of willpower.

I keep lists nearby of all that I hope to achieve during the day. I mark them off as I go and I tally them up at the end of the day to see if I accomplished them. In his book 'The Power of Less' Leo Babauta says that by limiting yourself to the essentials in business and in life, you stay on task more, get more thing done and improve the quality of life. I tend to agree. I hate getting to the end of the day thinking I didn't achieve very much. So keep an eye on your distractions by writing down every time you find yourself wandering away from your tasks. Ask yourself if it's because you're bored, or you're not being mentally challenged. Don't allow others to distract you. When someone interrupts you during something you're focused on, gently send them away. Set yourself some boundaries that will help you get the work done, and make it clear to other what they are. We are all entitled to our own space. Frequent interruptions are not helpful. Frequent suggestions from well-meaning colleagues, relatives or friends are not welcome unless invited in. Staying free from distractions is a choice you make and the price you pay for achieving results in your life.

So start with figuring out what's important. What do you really want to be doing with your time? What do you want to accomplish?

Examine your commitment to the task. Is it something you want to be doing, or are you just filling in time, or doing this out of sense of duty. If this is meaningful work, then you need to make a commitment to following through with it.

Don't fill up your days with too many things to do. This is a sure-fire way of bringing in some distraction. Cut your to-do list down to three or four things that you want to achieve by the end of the day.

Leave space in between to Twitter, chatter, or coffee break. You don't want to be nose to the grindstone all day. There is a time and place for everything, but set a timer on how long you want to be frittering your time away. And don't forget to leave time to do NOTHING. What an idea that is for us ABC types. I find that extremely hard, so I compromise with reading time. It's my time in the morning for catching up with some inspirational, or philosophical reading. I allow my mind to float. It feels good. Sprinkling your day with pleasures is just as important as getting the work done, so make time for that.

Being distracted can be a pleasure, but mostly it just stops you from getting where you want to go. If it's fear of failure that's holding you back, think about what you are most afraid of? Most people are more afraid of success than failure. If you truly succeed at what you are doing, how much better will you feel when you reach your goals. Stay with the positive. Stay focused and you will get where you want to go.

Tales from the Trail
"Safe and Predictable Didn't Work For Me"
—Dr. Susan Meyers

For most of my career, I fit myself into the narrow mold of public service. My first job was with the State Employment Service, and, except for brief breaks for graduate school and nine months with a private employment agency, I spent 33 years in a variety of settings related to municipal government. Safe and predictable choices, all of them, from child welfare and pre-school through citywide training. Some of my choices provided challenging projects; others paid the bills. Sometimes I was overjoyed, but somewhere about the 20 year mark I started to become restless and wondered if there wasn't more out there someplace. Still, I had great benefits , a good pension, and a salary that was increasing on a regular basis. Who could walk away from that?

I made one final switch—into management within the country's largest public transportation system. And by the end of the first day, I knew I had made a big mistake. But the pay was good, I liked my manager, and also, there was the security of those great benefits and just another 10 years to reach safety of a pension check. Besides, I was past forty. Who would want to hire me? I had worked in municipal government jobs forever. Would someone let me start over in private industry? Did I believe I could? Would anyone else believe I could? I was scared. So I stayed. And stayed. And stayed. Immobilized by my fear of the unknown.

In the year 2000, two things happened: I developed thyroid problems and I discovered coaching. With my thyroid in overdrive, I grew increasingly frenetic—starting as many new projects at work as I could possibly take on—and exhausted. I became a training machine, managing a small staff and starting up new initiatives for the organization. My group was training 25 managers a month in a two-week intensive seminar, assisting in the training of 50 supervisors a month in another two-week program, and creating a new program for executive managers. I arrived at work early, left late, and collapsed in an exhausted heap when I got home. It was a plan made for someone like me—at that point in my life—because it left no time for me to think or confront my fears.

Then, I discovered coaching. One free seminar and I was hooked. I loved it because it all felt very natural. I knew that I had been coaching my entire career and that pretty soon I was going to have to make it official. But "pretty soon" could have gone on forever. It was a little like when the White Queen offered Alice a position as a lady's maid with strawberry jam every other day. When Alice responds that she doesn't like strawberry jam, the White Queen reassures her that this will be no problem—it's always today, so every other day never comes. So, as long as I lived in my nice, safe, "pretty soon" sanctuary, I would never need to take action.

When I became so ill that I couldn't stop my hands from shaking and I couldn't walk without a cane, I had to take a few days off for medical treatment. I had to keep my life still. And in that stillness, it became clear to me that—benefits or no benefits, pension or no pension—my job was killing me, maybe not *physically*, but certainly *mentally*. In June of 2000, just a month shy of my 55th birthday, I quit my job. I had no pension, no plans, few savings, and only the promise of a part-time job and the vision of myself as a coach.

There was no flash of magic in these actions, only the magic of feeling the fear and doing it anyhow. I had sleepless nights. I doubted my sanity. But I never looked back. When I got scared, I told myself to get over it. At times I had no idea where my next check was coming from; even so, I was never happier. *I was free.* I was creating something that I wanted for myself instead of sitting at a desk resenting everyone and everything. A very important part of my inner self was coming alive for the very first time. This was my turning point, my revelation.

After such a fundamental change in my life's direction, every-thing was difficult at first. It took years to create a sustainable business. I almost gave up in 2001 when I quit my part time job the second week of September, only to have the entire city come crashing down around me in the form of several personal crises.

My practice continues to grow as my skills broaden and deepen. I am much more confident now. I no longer take on work out of fear that nothing else will come, and I finally managed to break that six-figure barrier. I love my life and I accept the fact that fear will always be present—sometimes acting as a roadblock, sometimes just whispering a small warning that may inform my choice, sometimes energizing me, but never paralyzing me like before. I have accepted fear as my friend, not my master.

Stepping Into the Jungle

Ask Yourself:

Where in your life are you ready to give up control?

Where in your life do you allow others to control you?

Do you spend a lot of time watching television instead of learning something new, or going out into the world? Where do you get distracted?

What plans have you formulated since you began this book?

What areas of your life would you like to change: Your body, your work, your relationships, your health or your money? Why?

Do you believe you are capable of doing anything you want to do, provided you want to do it badly enough? If so, what does that look like?

Notes

CHAPTER 18
Assume Your Dream

ᛧᛧ

"Daring ideas are like chessmen moved forward; they may be defeated, but they start a winning game."—Goethe

Start to believe in your dreams. It is your only hope for the future. Without them life is humdrum and boring.

Define Your Dreams

Everyone has dreams. Even those women who tell me they don't have any dreams. I know they all dreamed about something they wanted, someone they wanted to be, something that was far beyond their present state. It is the human condition to hope and wish for something better. You dream to escape, to enrich, and to fulfill your greater self.

I began to ask myself: What happens when I tell the truth about myself? What will success feel like? What if I'm far more intelligent than I give myself credit for? What if I make loads of money? What if I took total responsibility for my life? What if no one can blame anyone else for the things that are wrong?

What if each person discovers just how magnificent they truly are?

Looking back upon my life, this redefining process has taken place several times. From the lowlands of Scotland to the buzz of London, all the way across the Atlantic and the United States to San Francisco, then on to Los Angeles, Paris, Amsterdam, and New York; I have found pieces of myself along the way, and stepped up to the challenge of *Who Are You?* The flame inside will not be dampened once it has been lit.

Embarking on this journey requires each of you to admit that you have let fear divert you from your true purpose. You have given fear the power to control you and make decisions that take you further from your dreams. In some cases, fear has actually inhibited the ability to dream at all. Survival has been the focus…until now.

This is your time.

This *is* your time.

This is **your** time.

This is your ***time***.

This is your time!

Look into the mirror and repeat this line with the stress on each word in turn, and then all of them at once. Like the inner flame you carry, it intensifies and becomes more urgent, more powerful, and more true.

It's time to take the helicopter ride, to soar above the jungle and look at your life from a new perspective. You are in control. You can reinvent yourself.

If you could create the life of your dreams, what would it would that look like?

Throughout this book, I've urged you many times to get specific. This is the key to forging a path through the jungle. When you engage your five senses to create your dreams, you are already making them a reality. So write down where you are now, and where you want to be. That's your dream.

Now figure out a way to make it happen.

Marcia Wieder is the author of *Making Your Dreams Come True*. She says, "Dreams answer the question, "How do you want your life to be?" So describe your dream in as many ways as possible by asking yourself questions like: what are you doing in the dream, where are you doing it, how do you feel, how do you look, who are you with, and what are you creating or accomplishing. Next, ask yourself what is stopping you from achieving your dream. What beliefs are holding you back, and what do you need to change to fulfill your dream. Write it all down. That's your dream and no one else's so you can be as free with it as you like. Then ask, are you committed to making this dream a reality? If you are, then move to the next step.

"There is always an enormous temptation in all of life to diddle around making itsy-bitsy friends and meals and journeys for itsy-bitsy years on end....I won't have it. The world is wilder than that in all directions, more dangerous and bitter, more extravagant and bright. We are making hay when we should be making whoopee; we are raising tomatoes when we should be raising Cain or Lazarus."—Annie Dillard

Refine Your Dreams

The universe is an amazing place. It is vast, it is unknowable, and it is divine. It exists beyond any conscious ability to see it, but it is there. It is the stuff of dreams.

I am a great believer in the laws of attraction, which I intuitively understood long before I studied the principles. We used to say, *What goes around, comes around*, and I have done my best to live my life from as good a place as I can because I do believe that; and I also believe the words in the Bible: "As you sow, so shall you reap." These are the laws of the universe in action. Scientists call it cause and effect. Jung called it synchronicity. Recently, Rhonda Byrne called it *The Secret*. There have been many teachers of this principle. Napoleon Hill's *Think and Grow Rich* is the seminal book on changing your mindset. Ernest Holmes' *Science of Mind* is another important body of work. I recently saw Dr. Wayne Dyer who said something I have always believed—"you are connected to the divine and if you live life on a low frequency you will get mediocre results."

If you live life at a higher frequency, then you attract only the best. There are many such authors who have explored the relationship between our mind and the circumstances of our life. The basic principle is that the universe does not withhold, judge, or limit. You do that to yourself. Your dreams are limited only by how far you are willing to reach.

No matter what you call it, there is a divine force at work in life that has an amazing ability to manifest opportunities and positive affects, as well as attract the negative stuff you want to avoid if that's all your thinking. When you change your thinking, you will change your life. There is nothing in the universe that says you can't have what you want. The Secret is very simple. When you get clear about what it is you want, and start moving the fears and doubts out of the way, you can make it happen. It's not complicated.

Everyone has the potential in their lives to live their dreams.

The circumstances of my life buried those dreams for a long time, but in my forties, I decided to find out for myself what happened to the dream. I took a risk and told everyone I was going to be a writer. Until that moment, the most I had ever written was a soup cookbook and a short story of no more than ten pages. I joined UCLA's respected writing program and began to develop my skills.

There are no magic bullets. Everything in life is learning. If you are prepared to do the work, all things are possible. By the time I was forty-three, I had completed my first manuscript. It wasn't bad. I had some talent, but it was mostly determination that helped me succeed.

My dreams have taken me further than I could ever have imagined possible. When I was growing up, I dreamed of having my own little bungalow and enough money in the bank to pay my bills. That was the extent of a ten-year-old girl's dream. By the time I was twelve, I was dreaming about traveling overland to India. I wanted to see the world. My mind was a long way from Edinburgh, Scotland. At age sixteen, I would stand in front of the best department store in town and dream of affording the beautiful clothes, expensive makeup, and a glamorous life. By nineteen, I was pregnant with my first daughter, living in a basement bedsitter in London, and dreaming of Kensington Gardens and Peter Pan nannies who strolled with their children in elegant prams.

When I was twenty-one, I dreamed that I could get a college degree and teach kids in challenging neighborhoods. By twenty-three, I had my second child and at twenty-six I was divorced. By twenty-eight I was ready to depart London for California and leave it all behind. I was in search of a dream, but I didn't really know what that dream looked like.

When I arrived in California in 1979, I met my husband of twenty-nine years and counting. He introduced me to dreams I had never even considered. World travel (but not India!), fine dining, beautiful homes, and a wealth of experiences I had imagined, but was not convinced I could ever have.

Buried underneath all the good time, however, was my belief that I didn't deserve all this wonderful stuff. I believed I was really a loser. I was too busy judging myself to notice just how fortunate I really was. I didn't trust that I deserved this bounty, and I found a million ways to try and sabotage my good luck.

When I turned fifty, I wanted to fulfill the twelve year old's dream of going to India. Instead, I went to Bali and another dream became manifest. I'm still waiting to go to India, but there is plenty of time. Maybe when I'm sixty.

In so many ways, my life has been filled with extraordinary choices, and I am deeply grateful for all the opportunities I've had to express them. But more importantly, as I searched for the answers, as I dreamed the dream and was guided by it, I allowed other parts of the dream in that I never considered. Being open to new things gives you the opportunity to expand your dream beyond anything you would have thought possible.

Accept Your Dream

When you define, refine and accept your dream, you are creating your own reality. You are living your best life now. Doubts and fears will vanish, and if they occur, you will have a strategy for dealing with them. Remember, being fearless is the choices and decisions we make when fear shows up in our lives. When you accept your dream as a reality, you are already in it. It doesn't matter if the house hasn't manifested yet, or the bank balance is still on the low side. You are committed to your journey and will do everything in your power to make it happen. You will take risks, step outside the comfort zone, and create another one, because that's what life is all about. We are constantly recreating each day. We shed millions of layers of skin during our lifetime. We lose and regenerate millions of brain cells. We are reinventing ourselves every 100 days or more as our cells renew, we shed hair and grow more, our nails grow, and our blood purifies. Nothing is static in the body, nor should it be in your mind. You may not have control over your body and what it does automatically, but you can control your thinking if you want to.

We are all products of our dreams, no matter how inconsequential you think they may be. If a noose is leading you through life, know that you have made that choice. If you look back on your life and see how far you've come and realize that at some point you accepted the dream and made it a reality, then congratulations. That's what creating your best life is. You're doing it.

Tales from the Trail
"The Dark Deep Hole"—Jennifer Carter

When I was five, my mother left my father and I was no longer allowed to see him because he was – according to her – "abusive" and 'dangerous." But I was allowed to spend time with a man who became my stepfather. His name was Carl, and apparently he had decided long ago that little girls were far more interesting than grown women.

Carl gave me more attention than he gave my mom. We 'played' together often ('play' was the verb he used), until one day his play came to an end when my mother said, "Jennifer, how would you like to see your dad again?"

"Yippee!" I thought because despite all the "danger" I missed him.

The next day, my brothers and I were bundled into the car and we drove eight hours to my father's house. I wouldn't hear from my mother again for three years, until one day she appeared and whisked us off to Montana because she had heard he was 'abusive' again (he was not). I had only enough time to throw some clothes in a bag.

I lived with her for four years in several different homes, during which Carl left her. One day she said "I can't handle this place anymore," and left. She packed her bags, told me to tell my step brothers that she loved them, and left at night while everyone but me was sleeping. I was twelve; my youngest brothers were four, five and six. None of us would ever live with her again.

My brothers and I moved from family member (dad, step-dad) to family member, to friend of the family or members of the church, until we were adults. Most of my six brothers got into trouble in school. They were taking drugs, involved with gangs, and were in and out of juvenile hall. Two became teenage fathers. My oldest sister, who escaped the family early, graduated from UC Berkeley with honors at age 19. One older brother stayed clear of trouble and did well with his life, becoming a pharmacist. The rest all stumbled down less desirable paths.

As for me, despite the ups and downs, I graduated college with both a Bachelor's and Master's degree. I started several programs that empowered others to reach beyond their boundaries and I now run a coaching program for a world-class speaker, and I am a world-class speaker and writer myself.

My mission is to ensure that no woman ever has to feel stuck like I once did, afraid she has no options and feeling like she is that dark, deep hole of hopelessness and despair I once felt I was in. No woman should ever feel that 'she's not good enough" or that she "doesn't have what it takes" to make it.

How did I pull myself out of the dark deep hole?

I had people looking out for me. Friends who told me I was pretty, even if I didn't believe it, and friends who told me I could do better than all this and I could get myself to a better place. Thanks to them, I now have many people like that in my life.

Second, I decided that I did want something better and I started believing that I actually deserved it. I decided what I wanted for myself, and started going after it. I learned to model myself on successful people.

Third, I learned to push past the fears…
Past the fear I wasn't worthy.
Past the fear I wasn't good enough or smart enough.
Past the fear of "Well, you've failed in the past…what makes you think you'll succeed this time?"

Displayed on my wall is a big poster with the following words:

Feel the Fear And Do It Anyway™

Most people who knew me growing up would say I was too shy to be a public speaker and I had nothing to speak about anyways…but now I'm speaking all over the world and showing others how to get their message out and I have achieved a six-figure income and more.

I learned how to start *Living* fearlessly.

Stepping into the Jungle

Ask Yourself:

To create the life of your dreams, what would it look like? Be specific.

Who is in your dream with you? How do you feel, how do you look, who are you with, and what are you creating or accomplishing?

Write your dreams as if you were living it today. What does that look like? Be specific.

What actions are you taking to make your dream come true?

What do you need to change to fulfill your dream?

How committed are you to making the dream a reality? What will you do next?

Notes

CHAPTER 19
Act With Purpose

᙭᙭᙭

"Life is either a daring adventure or nothing at all."—Helen Keller

Believe you can do anything. Then see what happens.

Act 'As If'

Wayne Dyer said, "Stop acting as if life is a rehearsal. Live this day as if it were your last. The past is over and gone. The future is not guaranteed."

But there is another side to acting 'as if'; it's the trying things on for size part of life. It's one way of giving yourself permission to see if the dream is what you want. How does it feel when you role play what you want? Where do you need to tweak the process so you can get comfortable in your own skin. I acted 'as if' I was already a successful public speaker and best-selling author, and in my mind, I am, so it's only logical that the reality will take shape. Gradually, your life will change as you make these incremental shifts in your belief system.

As you start to imagine, then you become the person you want to be. To do the job you want to do. To have the kind of relationship you want. We put money in the bank to the value of what we desire. We are all capable of great wealth. These are all the ways in which acting 'as if' becomes your best life.

It's not a case of 'just believe'. The *as if reflective process* is an integration of Alfred Adler's ideas on individual psychology and Hans Vaihinger who developed the philosophy of "As If", which proposed that man willingly accept falsehoods or fictions in order to live peacefully in an irrational world. And while this may feel like pie in the sky, acting 'as if' has been shown to have an impact on the end result.

Ask yourself

◊ If you were acting 'as if' you were the person you would like to be, how would you be acting differently?

◊ If you were watching a videotape of your life, what would it look like?

◊ If a good friend would see you several months from now and you were more like the person you desire to be or your situation had significantly improved, what would this person see you doing differently?

When you act 'as if', you are programming your subconscious to accept your behavior, your thoughts, and your feelings as natural and normal for you.

Thomas Troward, an early 20th century Science of Mind proponent said, "the activities of mind draw into a man's life that which he considers normal for him, rather than that which he vaguely hopes or wishes for. When we believe our dreams are possible, when we believe we are capable of producing from our imagination, then we will create the life we want because we believe all things are possible."

When you act 'as if', you subjectively create a new "normal" for yourself.

Acting as if keeps you focused on your desire. It keeps you confident in its demonstration. It diminishes doubt. It strengthens belief and faith. You might say it even fools your subconscious into accepting without question what you want to happen.

Acting 'as if' allows you to bring your ideas into the physical world.

Say What You Mean and Mean What You Say

"A man does not know what he is saying until he knows what he is not saying."—G.K. Chesterton.

Do you always say what you mean, and mean what you say? Probably not. We all say things we don't mean, and frequently don't come out with the honest truth because we're afraid of rejection or hurting someone's feelings. You may also not say what you mean because you're afraid to ask for what you want.

One of my biggest hurdles I faced in starting my company was asking people for their business. Cold-calling prospects would send me into hiding. Until one day I realized that it wasn't about me, it was because they had no need for my services. Whatever it was I had to offer wasn't what they were looking for. This was a big Ah-Ha moment that allowed me to put myself forward without fear of rejection.

In relationships, we want our partners to love us so we stifle the impulse to speak our mind about inconsistencies that bother us, for fear we will be abandoned, get into an argument, or they will withdraw from us. In conversations with my husband, I would do a dance around a subject when I wanted something, because I wasn't sure he would give me it. I often used phrases like 'maybe, if is okay with you' in order to set up the scenario, or I would say' if you don't want to, don't worry, it's not that important,' while feeling that I was selling myself out. I wasn't coming right out and asking for what I really wanted. I had put myself in the role of the child asking of a parent, instead of acting like an adult and taking responsibility for what I wanted and accepting the outcome.

We decline to say what we mean regularly in our businesses because we don't want to offend, or because we're not sure and don't want to look foolish or ignorant, or perhaps because we don't want to lose our job.

Saying what you mean is living authentically. It is the place where you express what is most important to you, and you are willing to take responsibility for whatever the outcome may be.

As a mother, I know only too well when I discipline my children by withholding something, an hour later I've forgotten what I've said and give them exactly what THEY want. Saying you won't do something because you know it's not good for you, is great, but you'll go do it again anyway. Meaning what you say takes courage. This is especially important when you're making change in your life.

We disappoint ourselves constantly when we go back on our word. For example, if I decide to go on a diet, I'll tell myself I won't have any more cookies for a month, or I won't drink any wine for a month, and three days later, I've already gone back on my decision. There are thousands of ways in which we don't live up to our commitments to ourselves.

Saying what you mean, and meaning what you say is powerful and commands a great deal of respect. How many people do you know who live their life that way? Do you admire them for their ability to come right out with it, and then follow through without worrying about the outcome? I know I do.

Living authentically means living life on your own terms. You are not giving away or selling yourself short. You stand up for what you believe in. Are you ready to do that?

NO is an option!

Each day, millions of women around the world ask permission to live their lives. Many of them are passive, subjugated, marginalized, threatened, submissive, controlled and diminished.

Raised to believe from birth that their entire purpose in life is to serve others, they buy into the myth and swallow whole their frustration and depressions.

They are the victims of their own belief system and they are afraid to take on the responsibility of taking care of their own lives, making their own choices and making their own decisions.

What happens to young girls growing up? What happens to their power, their ability to make their own decisions, to take action based on their needs first without consulting others? How do women come to believe that their needs come second to everyone else's? How do women lose sight of who they are in relationship to others? When do women get to KNOW that they have the power to say NO and not be afraid of losing something.

These are the questions I've been asking myself for many years. I watched as my mother was dominated by my father both verbally and physically, and I watched as she struggled to find a voice and failed because she didn't believe it was possible.

I watched myself struggle to find anyone who would love me to make me feel whole, and I willingly allowed myself to put their needs before mine because I didn't know what it was I wanted.

I made huge mistakes with my children not knowing if I really wanted to be a mother, or even if I could be a mother, and then I invested myself in them so much that I lost sight of what was good for them. And I still did not know what I wanted.

I blamed others for what was lacking in my life. They were the cause of my lack of choices, my lack of opportunity, my lack of an independent life that seemed impossible to achieve while under the yoke of other people.

I wanted to KNOW who I was, and I wanted to KNOW what I was capable of.

I did not understand that the choice was mine. The power was mine if only I would take responsibility for my own decisions. I had to find my NO because I did not understand I was setting a very bad precedent for my children.

My children came to expect that I would always be there for them. My husband came to expect that I would cook, clean, take care of the children, and attend to their physical and emotional needs, and his also. After all, he was paying for it, wasn't he? I hadn't earned a penny in twenty years and therefore the financial control was his. I had given my life over to taking care of our two daughters, his daughter from a previous marriage, and the demands of a twenty-four/seven relationship that expected me to be there when he needed it. And he was needy. Any rejection of his wants was a rejection of him. Any selfish act on my part was an abandonment of the relationship we had created. We had an unwritten agreement that went roughly along the lines of "I'll cook, you clean", but I'll tell you what it is I want to eat.

I didn't have the courage to say **NO**.

Conflicts arose because I could never say what it was I wanted.

Instead, there were nagging, complaints, avoidance of sex, frustrated outbursts of anger, and lots of tears. My unspoken needs and fear of being rejected or abandoned complicated my relationship because I couldn't figure out how to tell him what it was I needed. Words like freedom to be myself were empty because I didn't know what that meant.

"You want to go out more often by yourself?" he would shout, "Go!"

I would retreat.

"You want to spend how much money? Do you really need it?"

I would withdraw.

"You were gone a long time. Where were you?"

And the stories would begin.

"Did you do what I wanted you to do?"

And the answers would come back a lie because I didn't want him to be angry with me because I hadn't done what he needed. I didn't want to risk the unpleasant feelings that it would generate by not doing what he wanted.

"I'll be away for a few days, but could you take care of this list for me," he would ask, as if I had a choice.

Then he would be gone, but not before he had called to tell me there was something else he had forgotten for me to do and I would add it to my list while cursing under my breath.

It wasn't enough that I was there taking care of the household details, making sure the children had what they needed, and being available at night after a long, tiring day.

I was Dr. Mom, PTA Mom, birthday party Mom, Gourmet Cook Mom, and nurturing, sympathetic Mom, who occasionally turned into Gremlin Mom, Freddie Kruger Mom, Hysterical in your face, don't touch me, don't ask me, don't breathe on me, Mom. Can you, will you, I want you to, came with a silent NO!

I did it because I wanted to be the best Mom, the best cook, the best wife, and the best sport in the world. I didn't want to give anyone the chance to say you are no good and I didn't want to leave. It seemed my choices were limited.

I lived that way for the first forty-two years of my life.

Respect comes when you trust yourself to say NO and mean it.

You are respected for your integrity. You are respected for your strength.

When you say what you mean and mean what you say, your world expands and the opportunities increase. Trusting yourself to make the right decisions, the right choices, to know what is good for you takes experience. We don't acquire it easily.

There are too many years of listening to messages that were negative; too many years of listening to other people's opinions about who they thought we were.

Trusting yourself is knowing yourself. Knowing what happens when you have followed certain paths and failed. Knowing what happens when you do something right and you make progress. Trusting yourself is number one key to becoming successful.

Other people have their own agenda. You have yours. Understand what that is, and you are more than half way to knowing what works for you in the world.

Tales from the Trail
"My Victory"—Ann Fry

In June of 2002, my husband (of 25 years) had a major heart attack. We had been separated for about 6 months. After triple bypass surgery, he couldn't go back to his apartment alone, so I took him to my place and nursed him through the start of his recovery. It was a bittersweet experience. If only we could have gotten along like that in our marriage—no arguing, no resentments, just loving and caring and healing.

After a week at my place, he left. We kept in touch for a while, but soon he drifted away and had less and less to do with me. I expected this to some degree. After all, I had left him in the first place.

Fast forward to Fall of the same year. It was a Saturday afternoon. I had been to a movie with my friend, Linda. We had come back to my apartment to hang out and for girl talk. There was a knock on the door. I opened it and it was my son Gabriel with my ex-husband. They were in the neighborhood and decided to stop in and say "Hi." They were happy to see Linda. We all sat in my living room, talking and laughing.

I have no clue what I said, but something triggered in my husband, and he screamed, "That's what you always did when we were together. You're nothing but a _____." He spewed out a litany of profanity, and he obviously didn't care who was there to hear it.

I was baffled and speechless. I reverted back to my standard response: my deer-in-the-headlights demeanor. With tears welling up in my eyes, I sat there silently, trying not to cry. During our marriage, this had been common, but usually it happened in private, not in front of Gabriel or friends. Our son listened and my friend watched in amazement. My response had always been the same—to capitulate and believe I was the one at fault, the bad person, the spouse in the wrong. Repeatedly, I had been reduced to smallness and misery and fear. His abuse had never been physical, but in many ways, being mentally abused is far worse. The scars go deeper. The pain is not on the surface and it never goes away.

Linda excused herself and left. Gabriel watched on in amazement. He had always known his father had a temper and could be abusive, but this was so unexpected. My ex continued to rant. Finally, I reached my limit. From somewhere deep inside, I mustered up the courage. I walked to my door, opened it, and said, "This is my house. You have no right to talk to me that way. Get out."

They left, and I slammed the door behind them.

I started to feel the impact and I began to cry—like I always had done. It was now time for me to curl up in a ball somewhere and feel bad about myself, but this time I did something entirely different: I got my purse and I left the apartment. I didn't let his abuse affect me the way it always had.

That was my victory!

During our marriage, I had always let him yell at me and berate me, and afterwards I would always feel diminished. Then I retreated into myself. But now, 6 months after having the courage to finally leave him (my first revolt), I had found even more courage to boot him out the door and not blink an eye.

A few minutes after they left, Gabriel called and said he had yelled at his father in the parking lot and told him to never speak to me that way again. So it was a victory for Gabriel as well.

During the time I was married to this man, I had always been very successful, courageous, and inspirational to others around me, while in the privacy of our home I allowed him to diminish me. When I finally found the courage to no longer accept his abuse, I was empowered to move beyond, to grow into a different person. Further evidence of this came four years later, when I moved from Austin to New York and rein-vented myself. I wrote a book and began what has become a successful career inspiring others.

Stepping into the Jungle

Ask Yourself:

By now, do you believe you can do anything you want to do. If not, why not?

Are you ready to try on for size the life you've created in your dream? If not, why not?

Are you creating the kind of relationship you want with another person? If not, why not?

Are you putting money in the bank to the value of what you've desired? If not, why not?

What would it take for you to truly create your best life now, this very minute?

What do you think is holding you back. Be specific.

If you were watching a videotape of your ideal life, what would it look like?

CHAPTER 20
Stay Confident

Please subdue the anguish of your soul. Nobody is destined only to happiness or to pain. The wheel of life takes one up and down by turn.—Kalidasa (4th century)

Confidence comes from knowing that no matter what comes up for you in life, you have the capacity to handle it all.

Who Are YOU?

You have walked through the jungle of your mind, confronted the difficulties and met the challenges and along the way discovered something wonderful.

Making decisions and doing so confidently brings your goals into focus. If you are clear about what it is you want, and who you are, then you will fulfill your desires.

When you know who you are, you feel good knowing you made a decision that benefited you. You feel good knowing that you are one step further on to a more positive future.

Life comes at you in increments otherwise you'd be over-whelmed. Confidence comes through experience and practice. The more you do it, the more successful you will be. You are empowering yourself with every small positive movement you make. Anything that makes you feel like you're giving to yourself without taking away from others will make you feel great. This is a fundamental principle in learning how to empower you.

The more you use that confidence, the more connected you will feel to the true and authentic you.

Start by taking small steps towards positive action in your life:

◊ When confronted with a choice, question whether it is good for you or not.

◊ When confronted with a decision, ask yourself what are the benefits of that decision.

◊ When you need an answer, find out what the question really is.

◊ When you are ready to blame, ask yourself what responsibility you had in the scene.

◊ When accused of something, ask yourself who is doing the accusing and see if there isn't something that isn't about you.

◊ When you are being judged, look to the source of the judging.

◊ When you need support, learn how to ask for it.

◊ When faced with an opportunity, will you take it or will you make excuses for not doing it.

◊ When faced with a choice, is it one that benefits you or benefits someone else, and if it doesn't benefit you, will you lose something by going ahead.

These are the small ways in which we can start to change the rules of behavior to benefit not only ourselves but the lives of the people we most care about.

We all benefit from our own empowerment.

You, your partner, your children, the world.

We are the best advertisement there is for the future.

A future filled with hope and a future in which we all get to live a life we want to live.

Living in harmony is not an impossibility. It starts with one person at a time and we build from there. We must start now. There is no later date. There is only now. If we start taking responsibility for our place on this planet and the future generations we produce, it will be an amazing revolution from within.

Most people work out of unconscious impulses and do not truly understand the impact of what it is they are doing. If we make a stand for our own selves, we are already challenging the status quo to deliver a better world.

We are stronger than we think. We are powerful in ways we can't imagine. We are the leaders of tomorrow and it with our strength the earth will heal itself.

We are the mothers and fathers of the world, whether we have children or not, it doesn't matter. We must take care of ourselves because no one else is going to do it for us.

We must learn to KNOW who we are.

No More Negative Self-Talk

You have come so far and yet you still hear the voices in your head that discourage and disparage. You still call yourself 'stupid' or 'careless' or 'thoughtless' instead of lovingly guiding yourself back onto the path you have chosen.

So I want to talk to you about Gratitude.

Be grateful that you are doing a good job. Doing a good job means you are succeeding in the world of your own making.

You can mark your successes by how many times you have taken the right decision for you. The changes you have made in your own life. That's how you mark your success.

You may remember that I asked you to keep a success journal by your bed each night. You wrote down in it everything little thing that felt like a success from that day. When you look back at these pages you will find enormous satisfaction in knowing that all these successes were a result of taking a decision and making a commitment to follow through.

That takes courage on a daily basis.

Remember 'feel the fear and do it anyway'. Fear can be crippling, but when you take action, it dissolves the fantasies that exist in your head, and right or wrong, most fear related items on the agenda are a result of a vivid imagination.

I can think of a dozen reasons why I should stop writing this book right now and put it away. There are too many books out there on the subject, there are many talented writers who have said the same kind of things I'm saying. It doesn't have enough credentials. It's just another silly self-help book. Those are the negative voices in my head. That's the self-talk I have to constantly guard against with an opposing argument. I refuse to let these voices of negativity stop me, because I know they are not my real voice speaking. My true, authentic voice says "so what. There are thousands of books out there, and I believe I am writing something that people want to hear in language that is readable and easy to understand." So I continue on, creating my world the way I want it.

Negative self-talk serves only one purpose. It keeps you from living your life the way you want to.

Learning to change your language will absolutely change your life. Turn off the Yadda Yadda radio; switch to a different channel. You can choose what you listen to.

Find Your Entourage

On this journey called your life, finding positive people is absolutely imperative.

Who do you want with you in the jungle? Someone who has already given up and is waiting to be devoured by a big cat? Someone who is so angry they keep chopping down the wildflowers with their machete? Or maybe you would like a pessimist who shakes his head and second-guesses your every decision. In this setting, it is easy to see the value of optimistic, supportive people in your life.

It is without question, the greatest gift you can give yourself.

All change demands support. I would not have made it this far without a team of phenomenal coaches, teachers, guides and therapists who helped me stay directed, adding valuable information to my knowledge base, and steering me clear of the quicksand that could cause me to lose direction.

This support team is a part of your journey. Do not think you can do it all alone. Remember the rhesus monkey experiment. We all need relationships. It is through them that we learn the most. They teach us, and we teach them. Be sure that you are attracting the right kind of relationships. If any are not fully committed to what you are becoming, then choose someone else. Life is too short to be limited by people and events that don't serve your needs.

You don't have to suffer under the pain of someone else's small mind, envy or jealousy. You have come too far on your path to settle for anything less than 100% support for WHO you are and WHAT you are creating in your life.

Each day of your life is an opportunity to surround yourself with people who will encourage and celebrate your growth.

Each day is an opportunity to embrace your true self.

Each day is a chance to look at your fears and make a decision to move forward and confront them.

Each day is a chance to truly live the life you want until the day you die.

Building your entourage is creating a strong, supportive network of people who share your dream and stand on the sidelines cheering you on.

You want to be excited about what you're doing so you can build excitement in other people. It's contagious. People want to be around others who are upbeat, focused and successful.

Positive excitement is infectious. It gets people going. It's what leadership is all about. Build your team of believers. These are your tribe. They believe in you because you believe in what you are doing. Every day.

You are respected and admired for your vitality. The word comes from life. To breathe it in, to move with a freedom you never felt before. To feel the difference that comes from being confident when you are with other people.

When you have more energy for yourself, you have more for other people. You become a beacon for other people because they want some of what you have. When people enjoy life they are fun to be around. When you have more energy, there is more to go around. Being depressed and anxious saps your energy. Being positive and filled with hope makes life so much easier to deal with. There are no problems too large.

Today, more than ever, the world needs change agents. People who are not afraid to do something different. Who are not afraid to stand up for what they believe. People who are making a difference in the lives of others.

You are creating change in your life and you will inspire others to change. That's powerful.

Tales from the Trail
"The Bliss of a Wanderer"—Claudia Scott

This story has become a family folk tale, one repeated over the decades, that elderly relatives swear really happened. It goes that in the rural New England town where they lived, there resided a middle-aged woman who never left her home. She was certain that if she did, she would die.

The lady's life was confined within the walls of her small house. One night there was a terrible storm, and as she hid under the covers of her bed a tree came crashing through the roof and she was instantly killed.

True or not, I love the moral of this yarn because it epitomizes the maxim that since you cannot escape your fears, you may as well face them and enjoy life to the fullest. It is a good fable.

There is another family story, however, that I know to be fact. It is the saga of a young woman named Karolina who was born in 1896 in a remote village in Poland. Growing up in a hut with only a wood stove and a dirt floor, it was a life of hardship and poverty. And although I know nothing about her youthful personality, I innately know that she had to be incredibly fearless.

When Karolina's older sister changed her mind about leaving the village to go to the United States because she had too much work to do as a seamstress (although I suspect that it was actually fear that held her back), Karolina agreed to go in her place. Since she was only seventeen, she also had to lie about her age to be approved for emigration.

All alone, with only one suitcase and a handmade quilt for her sponsor, this girl, who spoke no English, left the only world she had ever known. There were not even photographs to give her an idea of what she would be facing once she arrived in America. The only thing of which she could be certain was that, as she said farewell to her parents and siblings, she would never again see them nor her homeland. Ever.

When I contemplate the courage of her actions, I am often moved to tears. I try to imagine how confused her emotions must have been as she crossed the Atlantic in the steerage section of the SS Breslau.

Did she anticipate a wonderful new start in the land of opportunity or did she dread her decision to abandon the familiarity of her tribe, even as difficult and hopeless a life as it would have been for a bright young girl? Was she terrified? I sense that her loneliness had to be unbearable at times.

One of my greatest regrets is that I never asked these questions before Karolina, my paternal grandmother, died in 1972. Because of the language barrier, our personal communication was limited. As a young girl, I was also ignorant of the riches I could have received from her life stories.

Only once did we have a brief heart-to-heart chat. It was the week before I was going to Europe by myself as a spirited college kid. Bobcia said in broken English that I was a very lucky girl and that I had the whole world ahead of me.
As a twenty-year-old, I did not realize how prophetic and precious the statement was. But now, in my fifties, I cherish that golden moment. I also wonder if she was encouraging me

to become the torch-bearer for her own unrealized dreams. She, who never left the family farm after marrying and bearing twelve children.

Years later, when I did learn of her amazing odyssey, I instantly knew that Bobcia's spirit of facing the unknown had been transferred to my own essence. It clarified why I covet solo adventures. And just maybe, it explains the commitment I have made to strive to be fearless in a life with absolutely no guarantees. Karolina is not only in my genes and my psyche, but as I age, I also see more of her when I look at myself in the mirror, in my own face.

My mother said I first displayed a craving for adventure at age three, when I asked a visiting uncle, as he was leaving, if I could pack my luggage to go with him. This tickled everyone for several reasons. First of all, they didn't realize that I even knew the word luggage; second, I had never traveled anywhere during my short life; and third, I didn't own any luggage.

This was the foretelling, however, of a lifelong wanderlust and fearlessness. A passion for the world beyond my four walls, and an inherent knowing that I can handle what life presents, even if I, like the poor woman hiding under her covers, would rather not confront the storms of life when they happen.

When these challenges that the inspired writer Judith Viorst calls "necessary losses" do knock on the door, I often think of Karolina and remind myself that I too can face the uncharted future. I can deal with the pain and sometimes fear of not knowing what will happen next. I know that I come from strong stock.

And to keep myself from ever forgetting, I take an annual trek—alone. Not only for the pure joy of solo travel, but to also keep from ever becoming afraid of facing the world by myself. I choose a destination where I have never been, and for a week I reflect and renew and remember. It is a modern *vision quest* for a mid-life woman's spirit and soul. It is a sacred rite of fearlessness that I plan to celebrate until the time I am physically unable to do so.

And when that time does arrive, I want to know that I embraced the days of my life for all they had to offer. Without fear. Without looking back. To know that I continued the journey Karolina began so long ago.

> *"Fear is just a feeling. It is not a reason to stop, an excuse to fail, or a personal flaw. It is just a feeling and it cannot defeat you."*—Pema Chodron

Stepping into the Jungle

Ask Yourself:

Are you ready to be YOUR BEST SELF NOW? What does that look like?

Are you making choices and decisions that affect your life in a positive way? What is the difference between before you started this book and now?

When you are faced with someone's judgment about you, are you able to view the person who is doing the judging and see where it's coming from?

If you find yourself blaming someone, or something for what's wrong in your life, are you willing to take responsibility for your own part in it?

When faced with an opportunity, do you feel capable of making the right decision? If not, what would it take for you to do so. Who do you need to support you?

Are you getting the support you need? What does your ideal entourage look like? Name names, and start reaching out.

Notes

EPILOGUE

Throughout this book I have asked you some powerful questions to get you thinking about what you want to change in your life. Some of these questions have been hard to answer and some may need some time to put them into play. But throughout the book, I have done my best to offer you some guidance on the nature of change, and specifically, how to address the fears that are currently holding you back from creating your best life now. It has worked for me, and I know it can work for you.

Now, it's your turn. I hope you will use the information contained here to explore other options. There are many significant authors, speakers, teachers and leaders who are helping people like you move beyond the limitations of their lives so they can create a life of abundance, wellbeing and fulfillment.

At the end of the book you will find information on how you can take the teaching in this book to the next level with my Fearless Factor Home Study program. It will give you the tools and strategies you want to keep moving forward on the path you've chosen.

My hope for you is that you won't just put this aside and say, "Tomorrow." There is no better time than today to get started asking these hard questions. You already know what you have to do. The answers are already inside of you.

So take the risk. Respect your Intention and Show Kourage, so you can…

Be Fearless: See Where It Gets You!

To your great success
Jacqueline

The End of The Trail

It seems that every project I commit to becomes the beginning of my trail of adventure into the jungle of life. With sword in hand, I enter the jungle without a guide, trusting that my steps will be in the right direction to enjoy the journey. Throughout my life, I found you must be careful what you name your projects, as it will take you on the trail of that name. Fearless was the marker at this trailhead. I trusted that I would reach my goal of completion to success.

As a visual artist and photographer, I collaborated on a book entitled *Fearless Women: Midlife Portraits*. I intended that my photographs of fearless women, sword in hand, would dazzle the eye and inspire the heart. Little did I know the challenges that were ahead of me on the trail. With camera and sword in hand I braved a path that tested my mind, body and soul. Along the way, I learned to stand firm on my beliefs of how I wanted this book to be and I gained strength in my conviction. But the journey was arduous.

Half way through the project I was rushed to the hospital in agonizing pain. I was told that I had a tumor in my small intestines and they had to perform emergency surgery to save my life. I told the doctor that I couldn't possibly take the time for an operation as I had a book deadline, and couldn't we put it off until a later time. He told me that wasn't an option. I had 48 hours to have two feet of my small intestines removed or lose my life. So I surrendered.

I talked to my book agent the day after my surgery, and we both agreed that it would be almost impossible to finish the project on time. So I let go and trusted life. My trail had taken a turn and now I was to focus on resting and healing my body. Somehow in that moment of surrender I felt that it was all okay. Life was moving me along and I had no control and felt no fear.

Within four days after returning home, I was having my portrait taken with the sword. My makeup artist, Deva, said she would do my makeup in bed if it was more comfortable. My three photography assistants were excited to take turns creating an image of me wrapped in fabric, goddess like, holding the sword. I just had to have my photo taken. I wanted to document the staples down my belly that looked like a zipper. It was a challenge but an exhilarating one. Everyone that participated moved energetically together in a fearless dance.

By the end of that week, I was back at work photographing actress Kathy Najimy for the book. Rest, heal and photograph women was my life until the project was complete. I finished on time and the book was published. I took the risk, trusted myself, took sword in hand and slashed through the jungle to the clearing of success. It was the most amazing accomplishment of my life, so far.

It has been three years since my book was released, but my journey through the jungle was not over. Conflicts and challenges arose, and I began to hate the word "fearless." But I worked on finding patience and forgiveness in dealing with my writing partners and eventually declared, "I am a fearless woman." This has been my journey for the last few years to bring *Fearless Women: Midlife Portraits* to the world.

The book is a visual journal of my fearless healing. I see it in the faces of the women I photographed. But I did not do it alone. I had a strong, courageous team, especially my guide, my husband Joe, who sometimes fearlessly took his machete and forged ahead in the jungle cutting the vines away for me. What a blessing.

They say a teacher or a book will appear when the student is ready, The Fearless Factor is that book. Jacqueline's journey is inspiring. Her passion to share and teach her fearless message is powerful and direct.

"In our minds, there are no barriers except the ones we put there." That phrase stayed with me reading the "Fearless Factor." It brought me back to the journey I took making my book. As I reflected on the adventures on the trails through the jungle of my life, I have learned to move through fear to embrace courage.

This is an important book at this very fearful time in the history of our planet. With the current financial crisis, war and global warming, it is comforting to find a guidebook such as this. I don't know if fear is my friend yet, but I have learned to move through it and embrace my powerful ally, courage.

So here's to the fearless women in our lives! May we inspire each other to do great work in the world, play hard, laugh out loud, and sit in circles together. We are the healers of the planet.

I agree with Jacqueline that at the end of this lifetime I want to slide in sideways with a great glass of cabernet in one hand and chocolate in the other yelling, "Wow, what a ride!"

Exhale....

Mary Ann Halpin
Photographer of *Fearless Women: Midlife Portraits*
Author/Photographer of *Pregnant Goddesshood: A Celebration of Life*

Birth Is A Beginning
(anon)

Birth is a beginning
And death a destination
But life is a journey
A going—a growing
From stage to stage
From childhood to maturity
And youth to age.
From innocence to awareness
And ignorance to knowing;
From foolishness to discretion
And then perhaps, to wisdom.
From weakness to strength
Or strength to weakness
And, often, back again.
From health to sickness
And back, we pray, to health again.
From offense to forgiveness,
From loneliness to love,
From joy to gratitude,
From pain to compassion,
And grief to understanding—
From fear to faith.
From defeat to defeat to defeat
Until, looking backward or ahead,
We see that victory lies
Not as some high place along the way,
But in having made the journey, stage by stage.
A sacred pilgrimage.
Birth is a beginning
And death a destination.
But life is a journey,
A sacred pilgrimage
Made stage by stage
To life everlasting.

ABOUT THE AUTHOR

Jacqueline Wales is an author, speaker and coach of *The Fearless Factor*, a motivational company for people who are ready to turn off the fear, self-doubt and anxiety and turn on the confidence so you can live your best life now. Her unique programs have helped women around the globe develop strong personal success, confident communication and clear visions of their goals. She is also the author of a semi-auto-biographical novel *When The Crow Sings*, and recorded a CD of original songs written and produced by her called *Secrets of the Sun*. Jacqueline currently lives in New York City with her husband and their cute Coton de Tulear, Roxanne.

Jacqueline Wales is a gifted speaker with a timely message. For more information go to www.thefearlessfactor.com

The Fearless Guide To Living Your Best Life Package

Are you ready to banish your fears forever?

I am guessing you are because you have read this far.

Imagine yourself, 30 days from now…you look back after reading this book and the Fearless Guide, and you've applied everything you discovered in '***The Fearless Guide To Living Your Best Life Package***." With a warm heart, you realize the fundamental way your life has changed for the better. Everything you were afraid of or afraid to try before…seems so distant…and now you can't wait to start doing new things. In reality, it doesn't have to take you 30 days…you could devour every single word in a matter of days, it's really up to you to set your own pace.

In *The Fearless Guide* you will discover the path of success includes….

◊ The 'Mindset' of Being Fearless

◊ Evaluating Your Life By Defining Your Needs

◊ Finding Your Life Purpose

◊ The Building Blocks to a Better Life

◊ 50 Ways to Turn Your Life On

◊ 10 Ways to Get From Fear to Fearless

◊ 12 Key Habits to Create Your Best Life Now

◊ 25 Ways to Start a Conversation

◊ 5 Guaranteed Ways to Build Self Esteem

◊ 133 Questions To Find Powerful Answers

◊ And much, much more

PLUS 6 Hours of downloadable mp3's audio interviews to give you added insights into how you can obtain your best results and turbo-charge your learning process for faster results.

333

PLUS 30 minutes of coaching with Jacqueline to help you define your individual path and move you towards your desired results.

This is the program you want if you're serious about making changes in your life, are ready to be more confident, communicate more power-fully, and feel more self-assured than ever before.

If you are ready to create YOUR BEST LIFE NOW! The Fearless Guide to Living Your Best Life is yours for a special price of $97. (Normally the whole package sells for about $500)

And here's the super bonus... I GUARANTEE you will get results. If you don't, and you can honestly say the program has given you no value, you get to keep the program and I refund your money. I'm so sure that this material works, I'm willing to forfeit my materials so you can get what you need. You can't lose because i want you to win.

But before you go...

Don't buy this program if you are going to put it on the shelf and do nothing with it. That doesn't do you any good – that's shelf-help.

Don't buy this program if you are not ready to change behavior that no longer serves your needs – that's staying stuck in a rut.

Don't buy this program if you think it sounds like a good idea, but you're not committed to changing your life – that's called spinning your wheels.

Do buy this program if you are ready to start living your BEST LIFE NOW.

Go to http://www.yourfearlesslife.com TODAY and pick up your copy of the best gift you will ever give yourself. Guaranteed.

To your success,

Jacqueline *'FearCracker'* Wales

Dedicated to helping you overcome fear, self-doubt and anxiety – FAST!

P.S. Overcoming your fears, doubts and anxieties has never been easier. You can now turn them into confidence, success and finally live your best life now. I urge you to visit http://www.yourfearlesslife.com. It contains life-changing information for you. Sit down, close the door, take your phone off the hook, and invest the next 5 to 10 minutes discovering this information. **It's that important!**

The BAD news: You have reached the final page of *The Fearless Factor*, and if you've made it this far, you probably want more, but this is the end of this book!

The GOOD news: If you liked *The Fearless Factor*, you will enjoy my previous book, **When The Crow Sings**.

When the Crow Sings explores the history of mothers who abandoned their children, until one woman has the courage to break the chains of shame. In this Best-selling novel, three generations of women share a heritage entangled with secrets and unspoken sorrow.

Reader Review

"This is a powerful novel about three generations of women from Scotland, each one trying to carve out a life for herself, yet foiled and sometimes paralyzed by her family's history. For those who wonder "what does this novel have to do with me?" pick it up and you won't want to put it down. It is about the heartbreaking choices we make, about dreams that get cast away and then refound. The various plots are threaded together beautifully, and the pacing excellent. I am eagerly awaiting more writing from Jacqueline Wales. This one was on my top three for the year."—Adele Barker, Professor of Russian Literature, Arizona State University

Order Your Copy at www.TheFearlessFactor.com

Made in the USA
Charleston, SC
15 September 2015